PLANT PARADOX

Slow cooker

Cookbook

Top 2018 Healthy and Easy Lectin Free Recipes to Help Reduce Inflammation, Prevent Disease and Lose Weight

By
Laura Williams

Plant Paradox slow cooker cookbook

Copyright © 2019, By: *Laura Williams*

ISBN-13: 978-1-950772-42-1
ISBN-10: 1-950772-42-X

All Rights Reserved. No part of this publication may be reproduced in any form or by any means, including scanning, photocopying, or otherwise without prior written permission of the copyright holder.

Disclaimer:

The information provided in this book is designed to provide helpful information on the subjects discussed. The publisher and author are not responsible for any specific health or allergy needs that may require medical supervision and are not liable for any damages or negative consequences from any treatment, action, application or preparation, to any person reading or following the information in this book.

Plant Paradox slow cooker cookbook

Table of Contents

Preface 7
Introduction 9
   The Plant Paradox 9
   Are Lectins in Food Good or Bad for You? 12
   How to Avoid Lectin Poisoning? 18
THE PLANT PARADOX RECIPES 23
   Crockpot Spinach Soup with Cucumber and Basil 23
   Chipotle Black Bean and Quinoa Crock-Pot Stew 25
   RED BEAN, CHICKEN, AND SWEET POTATO SOUP 27
   Crock Pot Buffalo Chicken Lettuce Wraps 28
   Crock Pot Chicken and Chickpea Curry 30
   Crock Pot Honey Sesame Chicken 32
   Ingredients 32
   Slow Cooker Beef Manchaca 34
   Many Bean Crockpot Soup 36
   Overnight Slow Cooker Pumpkin Pie Steel 37
   Red Potatoes with Caviar and Cheese Recipe 39
   Salsa Crockpot Chicken 41
   Saucy Crockpot Beef 41
   Savory Crockpot Short Ribs 42
   Crockpot Poached Salmon 43
   Slow Cooker Momma's Roadhouse Chili 44
   Slow Cooker Thai Curry Ground Beef 47

Plant Paradox slow cooker cookbook

Slow Cooker Apple Cinnamon Oatmeal 49

Slow Cooker Balsamic Chicken 51

Slow Cooker Balsamic Chicken Wrap 53

Slow Cooker Bananas Foster 54

Slow Cooker Beef Stew 56

Slow Cooker Butter Chicken 58

Crockpot Black Bean Chili Recipe 60

Crockpot BBQ Pinto Beans 62

Crockpot Black and White Fondue 64

Crockpot Apricot Pork Sandwiches 66

Crockpot Cajun Pot Roast 68

Crockpot Caribbean Ribs 69

Crockpot Chicken Alfredo 71

Crockpot Chicken and Apples 73

Crockpot Cheesy Potatoes 75

Crockpot Chicken and Shrimp 77

Crockpot Chicken Cacciatore 79

Crockpot Chicken Sweet Potatoes 81

Crockpot Chicken Wild Rice Casserole 83

Crockpot Chicken Chili 85

Crockpot Chicken Chowder Recipe 86

Slow Cooker Cranberry Sauce 88

Slow Cooker Hearty Vegetable and Bean Soup 89

Slow Cooker Honey Bananas 92

Slow Cooker Herb Chicken and Vegetables 94

Slow Cooker Hot Chocolate Steel-Cut Oatmeal 96

Slow Cooker Home-style Potatoes with Garlic and Rosemary 98

Crockpot Italian Beef 100

Plant Paradox slow cooker cookbook

- Slow Cooker Lentil & Veggie Stew 102
- Slow Cooker Paprika Pork Tenderloin 104
- Slow Cooker Pomegranate Chicken Breasts 106
- Slow Cooker Pork Avocado 108
- Slow Cooker Pork Roast with Vegetables 110
- Slow Cooker Pork Tenderloin 112
- Slow Cooker Salsa Chicken 115
- Tex Mex Turkey Loaf 118
- Three Bean Cassoulet 119
- Three Ingredient Crockpot Turkey 121
- Turkey Breast Dijon 122
- White Beans and Sun-Dried Tomatoes 123
- Crockpot Greek Stew 125
- Crockpot Sausage Stew 127

BONUS RECIPES 129
- Applesauce Kielbasa 129
- BBQ Beef Crockpot Sandwiches 130
- BBQ Chicken Drummies 131
- Beach Boy's Pot Roast 132
- Cheesy Crockpot Chicken 133
- Crock Pot Cochinita Pibil 134
- Creamy Crockpot Potatoes 136
- Creamy Italian Chicken 137
- Crockpot Pork with Cabbage 139
- Crockpot Chicken Supreme 141
- Crockpot Sweet and Spicy Meatballs 143
- Crockpot Artichoke Spinach Dip 144
- Crockpot Beef and Black Eyed Pea Soup 145

Plant Paradox slow cooker cookbook

Crockpot Chili Beef Sandwiches 146
Crockpot Chili con Queso 147
Crockpot Chutney Ham 148
Crockpot Crab Spread 149
Crockpot Easiest Pork Chops 150
Crockpot Fish Chowder 151
Crockpot Fruited Pork 153
Crockpot Gingered Carrots 154
Crockpot Ham Lentil Stew 155
Crockpot Honey BBQ Pork and Carrots 156
Crockpot Honey Chicken and Dried Fruit 158
Crockpot Hungarian Goulash 160
Italian Chicken and Potatoes 163
Crockpot Italian Pork Chops 164
Chicken Tikka Masala Pizza 166
Crockpot Italian Sausage and Peppers Recipes 170
Crockpot Maple Glazed Turkey Breast 172
Crockpot Mexican Flank Steak 174
Crockpot Mexican Round Steak 176
Crockpot Moroccan Lentil Stew 177
Crockpot Onion Meatballs 179
Crockpot Onion Turkey with Stuffing 180
Crockpot Peanut Chicken 182
Crockpot Pork Chili 183
CONCLUSION 185

Preface

Most of us have heard about the gluten, whey protein, which causes a widespread inflammation in the body. Americans spend billions of dollars on nutrition without gluten to protect their health. But what if we lose the root of the problem? At the plant Paradox, Steven Gundry, a well-known cardiologist, finds that gluten is just a series of common and very poisonous protein plants called lectin. Lectins are found not only in cereals such as wheat but also "gluten free" foods that most of us consider to be healthy, including many fruits, vegetables, nuts, beans and conventional dairy products. After swallowing, these proteins cause some kind of chemical warfare in our body, which causes inflammatory reactions that can lead to weight gain and serious health problems.

In his only clinical course in California, Dr. Gundry successfully treats tens of thousands of patients with autoimmune diseases, diabetes, gut syndrome, heart disease, and neurodegenerative diseases detoxifying the cell protocol. hoses and nourishes the body. Now in Plant Paradox, it shares this clinically proven program with listeners from all over the world.

Introduction

The Plant Paradox

It's hard to turn on the television today, not to hear about "false news". The proliferation of produced "facts" and ignoring the truth is a great threat to our society. As others have already pointed out, for years we've been hearing fake news in consumer food-level messages. Regardless of the number of doctors per person: standing in front of the libraries of libraries is surely a way to feeling confused and uncertain.

Recently, the new book has attracted public attention, The Plant Paradox, by Steven Gundry, MD, focusing on the surprising claim that lectins are the source of most, perhaps all human diseases. It takes a long time to erase all the nonsense that affects the popular media in terms of eating, but we have received many questions about the book and its assumption that lectine are the true culprit of our zeal.

Dr. Gundry writes on his website: "I think I discovered unconventional truths about human nutrition." Unconventional? Yes, the truth? Not so fast. Plant Paradox writes an author who reminds us of his great career in medicine, including his research experience. Dr. Gundry says, "in all humbleness," that "has found that there is a common cause for most health problems" and that "it is based on extensive research, including [his] own documents, published in reviewed medical journals, but nobody has ever met "He says the so-called" health specialists "have stressed our laziness, fast food support, and so on. but to him, "Unfortunately, they are wrong … [and yes] … the real cause is so well hidden that you will never notice."

We seem to have discovered the incredible secret Dr. Gundry just discovered. So he wants to educate us, but what? The first track comes from the title of the book Plant Paradox. The reader might think, "Ah, maybe something is wrong with the whole grain, the absurd vegetables after all! I like it, I knew there was a reason why I never liked vegetables and why I would change, eat meat fed with grass! This book is for me!

So what's wrong with the plants? According to this book, it is not just the terrible gluten we have heard so much, but also the whole group of "highly toxic herbal proteins, called lectins," including gluten. He says that "lectins are not only found in cereals such as wheat, but also" gluten-free "foods such as fruits, vegetables, nuts, beans and conventional dairy products." consumption, "inducing the type of chemical warfare in our body, causing inflammatory reactions that can lead to weight gain and serious health problems."

Are Lectins in Food Good or Bad for You?

Lectins are guilty of a major "white bean incident" in Japan in 2006. On Saturday night, TV shows had a new weight loss method. The method was simple: fry the dry raw white beans in the pot for three minutes, grated beans and spread them over the rice. In a few days, thousands of patients have fallen, some of whom are suffering from diarrhea and vomiting so serious that they have ended up in the hospital. Future? Ledin poison.

Three minutes of dry heat are not enough to destroy the toxin cheeses in the beans. If you do not pack it, cook one hour of worms to completely destroy all lecithin, though, if you first sip it overnight, 98% of the lectin disappears after 15 minutes of boiling, all in half an hour. And, when they tried white beans, rubbing for three minutes did nothing; it is not surprising that people became ill while 95% of lectins were inactivated after three minutes of boiling and completely inactivated after ten minutes. Obviously, "Do not eat raw beans" is a traditional warning in Japan that [avoid] intestinal problems, "and now we know why.

While preservation can completely eliminate the most preserved beans, it is possible that some of the remaining activity of lecithin remains in cannabis beans, although it does not seem enough to cause toxicity, ironically, "lectin doses may be useful for stimulating bowel function, limiting tumor growth and improving obesity ". What is it? I thought the lectins were poisonous.

As long as people speculate that diet nutrition is harmful, others have assumed that they can be protective. "If this theory is correct, appropriate oral contraceptives should be useful in [preventing] (and possibly treating) colon cancer ..." Or, of course, we could eat our vegetables.
began to interest in the so-called "anti-tumor effect of herbal lectins" in the discovery of 1963, "... lecithin that could

differentiate between [cancer cells and normal cells]. "The general masses of researchers discovered the substance in wheat germ: the lecithin wheat in its entirety, it appears to be specific to tumor cells, pulled" tumor cells while normal cells "have remained almost completely alone. If you can specifically take someone's stool pattern, and depending on the lining of the colon for lining the cells that separate the chair, you can effectively predict the presence of polyps and cancer.

And later, it was discovered that lectins can not only distinguish these two, but quench the cancer cells, leaving the normal cells to a large extent. For example, it was found that the same white lecithin grain removed near-total cancer, head and neck cancer, liver cancer, breast cancer cells, and cancer cells (at least in most cases) from the cancerous carcinoma of the uterus in about three days. But it was in Petri's bowl. This is a largely exemplary basis for antitumor activity of herbal lectins: this study of Petri dishes. How do we know that dietary lectins are absorbed into the body?

Bowel cancer is one thing. I mean, the fact that lectins can kill colon cancer cells in Petri dishes can be applied because the edible foods can come in direct contact with carcinogenic or precancerous cells in our colon, "a mechanism [where bee consumption can prevent and treat colon cancer. "Or, more exciting, the potential for efficient cancer cell repair." [The loss of differentiation and invasion is [. ..] Highlights of the [tissue] malignant ", meaning that when a normal cell becomes cancer cells, the tendency to lose its specialized cancer cells breast function becomes less like a wing. colon cancer cells become less similar to colon.

And what these researchers have shown for the first time is that the lectin in the brain can take colon cancer cells and make them similar to normal cells. Here are the previous images: cancer cells develop only in amorphous groups. But then these same cancer cells are exposed to bean lectins after two weeks. The cells began to return to the growing glandular structure, like normal colon tissue. So, nutritional lectins, either putting them in a tablet or something "can slow the progression of colon cancer," which can explain why consumption of beans, peas, chickpeas and lentils seems to be reduced. [of] the risk of colon cancer, "based on 14 studies with nearly two million participants. Okay, but what does cancer out of the digestive tract?

"Although foods containing lectins [like beans and whole grains] are often cooked or processed, these treatments cannot always be avoided ... For example, lectins are discovered in peanuts" peanut butter and we try them It does not eat cooked but roasted or even raw Yeah, but can we absorb the lectures in our system Yes, the hour after eating raw or fried peanuts can reveal peanut butter in the bloodstream of most people It's the same with tomatoes Some unsightly lectures in However, wheat lectin, known as WGA, wheat germ with agglutinin, does not look like you get to our bloodstream and after obviously an equivalent of more than 80 sliced bread in wheat dairy, and if you eat something like pasta, boiling can boil the lecture in the first place.

In terms of phytochemicals in the fight against cancer, lectins can "resist digestion resulting in high biological", "which could allow" cellular mechanisms of hosts that use full potential in the fight against cancer ["dramatic"]. [the advantages] which lecturers have to offer. "However, these dramatic advantages have not been demonstrated in humans, but it seems, we know that population studies show that" dietary diet consumption is strongly associated with reduced risk of developing certain types of cancer, "

Now you could eat less carcinogenic. But plants have all these active components that appear to protect themselves from "initiation, promotion and [progression] of cancer." So maybe the lectins are one of those protective compounds. Look, we know that people who eat more beans and whole grains usually have lesser cancer in general; We do not know exactly why. Now, can you tell who knows? Who cares? Well, Big Pharma worries. You cannot earn as much money as healthy food as with lecture-based drugs.

How to Avoid Lectin Poisoning?

In the nineteenth century, a Wheat fusion was discovered, which will be known as the first in the class of lectin proteins, natural compounds found in food but concentrated in beans, whole grains and some fruits. Vegetables Every ten or ten years, in popular literature and medical literature, the question arises as to whether dietary diets are causing the disease. Lectin is easy to pick up the hysteria. After all, that he first found in 1889, he was called Ricin, known as the "powerful poison killer" used by the Kremlin to kill anticommunist dissidents, dishonest or chemistry teachers, as far as this is concerned. Ricin is a lecturer. Fortunately, "many lectins are not toxic, like those found in tomatoes, lentils ... and other common foods." Even those who are poisonous, like those in the beans, are completely destroyed by good cooking.

But you cannot eat raw beans. If that is the case, it will double the nausea, vomiting and diarrhea in a matter of hours, thanks to the lectures, which would otherwise be destroyed by good cooking. However, how do you eat raw beans? I mean, the only way they're selling without cooking is like beans, and they're like small stones. Well, in the first reported epidemic, "an improvisation dinner was done" with a bean bag thrown into a pot and soaked in the water overnight, but never cooked. You cannot just throw the beans into a slow cooker. Dry beans should be cooked. The beans must be soaked in water for at least five hours and then cook for at least ten minutes. Ten minutes? The beans will not be made in just ten minutes. Exactly. Yes, cooking with previously baked beans for a few minutes can ruin the lectin, but wait an hour before they are edible before they can easily level with the fork. Then, the lectins would disappear before they were acceptable.

Without prior sucking, 45 minutes in the pressure cooker are needed to remove all lectins, but one hour to make edible beans. So, basically, "[it seems] cooking beans to a point where they can be considered edible, it is more than enough to almost destroy any activity [lectin]". Even 12 hours at 65 degrees Celsius, however, is not like the temperature of a hot cup of tea. However, it can be said that they are not made, they are firm and elastic, although you can imagine putting them as a "raw" vegetable salad, and this could make people sick. And that was done, with dozens of incidents, all of which were "easy to avoid" if the beans were soaked overnight, dropped off and then cooked for at least ten minutes. Or, if they only eat canned beans. Grains are preserved beans; The process of conservation is the process of cooking. "None of the confirmed incidents [needed] in canned beans."

From the early 1960s, we know that "traditional cooking methods can effectively destroy the lessons in the beans and therefore it is possible to ignore any human problem associated with properly processed legume lectures." They can show that rats are not good for them or for cellular tissue in Petri dishes. But in these articles claiming that dietary diets can be "toxic and cause disease," the only negative effect they can find in humans are raw and insufficiently scraped beans. While dietary lectins cause disease, why not test this assumption, then " tested 24 domestic pigs, "and Paleo-Pig diet beaten pigs fed with grains. Cannot you find people ready to eat paleo?

In response to one of these examinations, it is mainly based on laboratory rodents, colleague review warned that we should not draw conclusions on the involvement of nutrition lectin causing "illness without a positive and final test," which has been written more than a quarter of a century before and this clinical evidence has not yet been materialized. What we have, however, is more and more evidence that legumes: beans, peas, chickpeas and lentils are good for us, associated with longer duration, significantly lower risk of colon cancer (one of the major causes of cancer). is considered part of "a natural, cost-effective solution without side effects for the prevention and treatment of [Type 2 diabetes]". Aléatoirez people eat five lenses of mugs, chickpeas, peas and navy beans a week, and you can see the same benefits in terms of weight loss and metabolic benefits with calorie intake control. A, the theory of complete lectins is based on the fact that foods containing the lectin are inflammatory.

But, prescribe four servings per week of legumes, full cheeses, and get a significant drop in the C-reactive protein; In fact, 40% fall in this main indicator of systemic inflammation, eating more beans.

The so-called "paradox of plants" is that, above all, healthy herbal foods are the foundation of good nutrition, but supposedly we should avoid beans, whole grains and some fruits and vegetables due to bad lectures. But if you look into science, all of the whole plant foods are associated with decreasing mortality, which means that as much as you eat, more people tend to live. And this includes foods rich in lectin such as whole grains and beans. So, maybe there are not really any paradoxes.

THE PLANT PARADOX RECIPES

Crockpot Spinach Soup with Cucumber and Basil

Ideal slow cooker size: 3 quart

Cooking time: 6 hours on low or 3 hours on high

Ingredients:

1 cucumber (peeled and cut into large slices)

1 Tablespoon of chopped dehydrated onion (or ¼ cup minced fresh onion)

½ teaspoon of pepper

2 cups of chicken broth (or better still 2 cups of water and 1 teaspoon of Shirley J Vegetarian Chicken Bouillon)

¼ cup of chopped fresh basil

8 oz. of fresh spinach (divided)

1 Tablespoon of olive oil

¾ teaspoon of salt

2 garlic cloves

½ cup of heavy cream (it is optional)

Directions:

1. First, you place half of the spinach (4 oz.) in the slow cooker.
2. After which you add in the cucumber, olive oil, onion, salt, pepper, garlic and broth.

3. After that, you cover and cook on LOW for 6 hours or on HIGH for 3 hours.
4. At this point, you pour contents of slow cooker into a blender (depending of the size of the blender you may need to do this part in batches).
5. Then you add in the rest of the spinach (4 oz.) and blend until smooth and creamy.
6. Furthermore, you pour blender contents back into the slow cooker.
7. After that, you warm the heavy cream and pour it in the slow cooker (Note: if you want the soup to be dairy free, I suggest you eliminate the cream).
8. Finally, you add in chopped basil and pour into serving bowls and then salt and pepper to taste, if needed.

Chipotle Black Bean and Quinoa Crock-Pot Stew

Ingredients:

1lb of dried organic black beans (rinsed and picked over)

1 (28-ounce) can organic tomatoes, diced

3 cloves garlic (minced)

1 red bell pepper (chopped)

2 teaspoons of Chile powder

¼ cup of fresh cilantro

sea salt and pepper (to taste)

1-2 dried chipotle peppers

¾ cup of uncooked quinoa (rinsed and picked over)

1 red onion (diced)

1 green bell pepper (chopped)

1 dried cinnamon stick

1 teaspoon of coriander powder

7 cups of water

Ingredients for topping:

Green onions, thinly sliced

Avocado

Cilantro

Lime wedges

Directions:

1. First, you load all of the ingredients, except the salt, into your slow-cooker.
2. After which you stir to combine (**NOTE:** If you wish to sauté the onion, garlic and bell pepper first, you can, but I like to make crock-pot cooking as simple and quick as possible.)
3. After that, you cook on high for about 4 to 6 hours, or on low for 8 to 10 hours, until the black beans are tender (The time to cook the beans can vary based on the strength of your slow cooker and also the freshness of your beans)
4. Then you add the salt at the very end, as it will affect how the beans cook, if you add it at the beginning.
5. Further, feel free to remove chipotles (if you don't want a mouthful of a whole spicy pepper) and the cinnamon stick before serving.
6. Finally, you ladle into bowls and serve topped with fresh cilantro, green onions, a squeeze of fresh lime juice, diced avocado, sour cream, hot sauce, tortilla chips, etc.

NOTE:

If your crock pot is known for not being very strong, I would suggest soaking and/or pre-cooking the beans first, before putting them in the crock pot.

However, older beans can take longer to cook, so that is also something to keep in mind.

Plant Paradox slow cooker cookbook

RED BEAN, CHICKEN, AND SWEET POTATO SOUP

Ingredients:

4 cups of sweet potatoes (peeled and cubed)

2 (about 14.5-oz) cans chicken broth

1 (about 10-oz) can no-salt-added diced tomatoes (undrained)

1 Tablespoons of Cajun seasoning

Fresh cilantro

2 (about 15-oz) cans no-salt-added red beans (rinsed and drained)

8 oz. of boneless, skinless chicken breasts (cut into bite-sized pieces)

2-1/2 cups of green sweet peppers, chopped (about 2 large)

One (about 10-oz) can tomatoes and chopped green Chile peppers (undrained)

2 garlic cloves (minced)

Directions:

1. First, you combine beans, sweet potatoes, sweet peppers, chicken, broth, diced tomatoes, tomatoes and green Chile peppers, Cajun seasoning, and garlic in a 5 to 6-quart slow cooker.
2. After which you cover and cook on low-heat settings for 10 to 12 hours or on high-heat setting for 5 to 6 hours.
3. Then you served topped with cilantro.

Crock Pot Buffalo Chicken Lettuce Wraps

Nutritional information:

Servings Size: 1/2 cup chicken + veggie
Calories: 147.7

Fat: 0.1 g

Carb: 5.2 g

Fiber: 1.6 g

Protein: 24.9 g

Sugar: 1.7 g

Ingredients:

Ingredients For the chicken:

One celery stalk

One clove garlic

1/2 cup of hot cayenne pepper sauce (I used Frank's)

24 oz. of boneless skinless chicken breast

½ onion (diced)

16 oz. of fat free low sodium chicken broth

Ingredients for the wraps:

2 large celery stalks (cut into 2 inch matchsticks)

6 large lettuce leaves (Bibb or Iceberg)

1 ½ cups of shredded carrots

Directions:

1. First, you combine in a crockpot the chicken, onions, celery stalk, garlic and broth (enough to cover your chicken, you can use water if the can of broth isn't enough).
2. After which you cover and cook on high for 4 hours.
3. After that, you remove the chicken from pot, reserve ½ cup broth and discard the rest.
4. At this point, you shred the chicken with two forks, return to the slow cooker with the ½ cup broth and the hot sauce and set to on high for an additional 30 minutes.
5. Then you make 3 cups chicken.
6. Furthermore, to prepare lettuce cups, you place ½ cup buffalo chicken in each leaf, top with ¼ cup shredded carrots, celery and dressing of your choice.
7. Finally, you wrap up and start eating!

Plant Paradox slow cooker cookbook

Crock Pot Chicken and Chickpea Curry

Ingredients

2-3 potatoes (cubed)

4 cloves garlic (minced)

2 tablespoons of red curry paste

1 teaspoon of red pepper flakes

½ teaspoon of freshly ground black pepper

1 (12.5 ounce) can chickpeas (rinsed and drained)

2 chicken breasts (cubed)

1 onion (thinly sliced)

1 (24-ounce) can tomatoes (whole, diced, crushed, whichever one you prefer – as for me I used whole and crushed them with the back of a wooden spoon)

1 tablespoon of curry powder

1 teaspoon of kosher salt

1 (1-inch) piece fresh ginger (grated)

4 leaves fresh basil, thinly sliced (or better still chiffonade, for you fancy folks)

Directions:

1. First, you throw all of your ingredients into the crock pot, then stir to combine.

2. After which you set it on high for four hours, or on low for eight hours.
3. Then when it's done, you add in the rinsed chickpeas, stir to combine, and let it sit for 5 minutes to heat through.
4. Finally, you serve alone, or with rice or pita.
5. Enjoy!

Crock Pot Honey Sesame Chicken

Ingredients

Salt and freshly ground black pepper

2 cloves garlic (minced)

2 Tablespoons of tomato paste

½ cup of low sodium soy sauce

¼ teaspoons of red pepper flakes

1/3 cup of cold water

1 green onion (sliced *for optional garnish*)

4 boneless chicken breasts

½ cup of diced onion

½ cup of honey

2 Tablespoons of apple cider vinegar

2 Tablespoons of vegetable (or canola oil)

4 teaspoons of cornstarch

½ tablespoon of toasted sesame seeds

Directions:

1. First, you place chicken in crock pot and season with salt and pepper.

2. After which you mix in a medium bowl, the onion, garlic, honey, tomato paste, vinegar, soy sauce, oil, and red pepper flakes thoroughly.
3. After that, you pour over the chicken and cover the crock pot.
4. At this point, you cook on low for about 3 to 4 hours or on high for 2 hours.
5. Then in a small bowl, mix the cold water and cornstarch to make a slurry, set aside.
6. Furthermore, you remove the chicken from the crock pot and place on a cutting board, leaving the sauce in the crock pot.
7. This is when you add the cornstarch mixture to the crock pot and stir to combine.
8. After that, you turn heat on to high and allow to cook until thickened, about 10 minutes.
9. While the sauce is thickening, I suggest you shred the chicken into bite sized pieces.
10. Finally, once the sauce has thickened, you place your chicken and pour sauce over it.
11. Then you sprinkle with sesame seeds and green onion.
12. *Make sure you serve with rice.*

Plant Paradox slow cooker cookbook

Slow Cooker Beef Manchaca

NUTRITIONAL INFORMATION

Serving Size: 4 oz.

Calories: 157.1

Fat: 4.4g

Carbs: 3g

Fiber: .8g

Protein: 24.9g

Ingredients

Salt and pepper

4 tablespoons of fresh lime juice

1 cup of red bell pepper (diced)

3 serrano chilies (stemmed, seeded, and minced)

½ teaspoon of dried oregano

3 pound of beef brisket (or better still lean rump roast, trimmed of fat)

2 tablespoons of Maggi sauce (a Latino seasoning) or better still 2 tablespoons of Worcestershire sauce

1 ½ cups of diced onion

3 garlic cloves (minced)

½ cup of beef broth

½ (14 oz.) can diced tomatoes with juice

Directions:

1. First, you season the beef with salt and pepper and place into the slow cooker.
2. After which you whisk together in a medium bowl, the lime juice, beef broth, and Maggi.
3. After that, you stir in the other ingredients and then pour over the beef.
4. Then you cook on low in the slow cooker for about 8 hours.
5. At this point, you shred the beef using two forks and serve.
6. As for me, I usually like to let the shredded beef hang out in all the cooking liquid/sauce for about 30 minutes before serving. Make sure you keep the slow cooker on low.

Many Bean Crockpot Soup

Tip:

Feel free to make this easy crockpot recipe using any mixed bean blend and just four other ingredients.

Make sure you use Hearty Bean Soup Mix for this delicious recipe.

Ingredients

2 onions (chopped)

1 teaspoon of dried thyme leaves

14 oz. of can diced tomatoes (undrained)

2-1/4 cups of Hearty Bean Soup Mix (without seasoning packet, or mixed dried beans)

10 cups of water (or better still chicken broth)

4 carrots (chopped)

Preparation

1. First, you combine all ingredients except for tomatoes and stir well to combine.
2. After which you cover crockpot and cook on HIGH setting for about 8-10 hours or until beans are tender.
3. Then you add tomatoes, stir, cover, and cook on high for 15-20 minutes longer until heated.

Overnight Slow Cooker Pumpkin Pie Steel

Cut Oats: With No Sugar Added

NUTRITIONAL INFORMATION

Serving Size: 1 cup.

Calories: 188

Fat: 1g

Sodium: 193 mg

Carbohydrates: 15 g

Dietary Fiber: 2 g

Sugars: 7 g

Protein: 1 g

Ingredients

7 cups of water (NOTE: almond or regular milk can be substituted)

2 teaspoons of vanilla extract

2 teaspoons of pumpkin pie spice

2 cups of steel cut oats

2 cups of canned pumpkin puree

½ teaspoon of salt

It is optional: 1 cup of honey or better still 4 teaspoons of vanilla liquid stevia

NOTE: Sweetener can be added during cooking or cook it without and each person can add their own sweetener of choice on top after cooking.

Directions

1. First, you combine all ingredients in your slow cooker and cook on low for 8 hours.
2. Enjoy!

Red Potatoes with Caviar and Cheese Recipe

Tip:

1. You can cook this potato in the microwave or baked in the oven.
2. Remember that this classy side dish is both low-calorie and low fat.

Ingredients

3 Tablespoons of Neufchatel cheese

1 Tablespoons of black lumpfish caviar

12 new red potatoes (about 1 pound), scrubbed

1 Tablespoons of low-fat (1 percent) buttermilk

1 teaspoons of chopped dill

Preparation

1. First, you place the potatoes in a single layer in a shallow microwavable container.
2. After which you cook on high for about 3 minutes until fork-tender.
3. Alternately, bake the potatoes at a temperature of 350 degrees for 20 minutes.
4. After that, you cut the potatoes in half; place, cut-side down, on a platter.
5. Then with the help of a spoon or a melon baller, make a small well in the top of each potato.
6. Furthermore, you mix in a small bowl the cream cheese and buttermilk until smooth.

7. Then with the help of a rubber spatula, fold in the dill and caviar.

8. Finally, you dollop about 3/4 teaspoon of the mixture into the well of each potato.

NUTRITIONAL INFORMATION
Serving Size: per serving.

Calories: 54

Fat: 1g

Carbs: 10g

Protein: 2g

Salsa Crockpot Chicken

Tip:

1. Feel free to use any flavor of your favorite salsa in this super easy and delicious recipe. (For me, I like the complex sweet and hot flavor of fruit salsas in this recipe).
2. The smaller grocery stores are carriers of fun flavors salsa.
3. You can serve it with Chili Rice Casserole to soak up the wonderful sauce.

Ingredients

6 pounds boneless, skinless chicken thighs

2 (16 ounces each) jar peach salsa

Preparation

1. First, you combine in a 3-4-quart crockpot and cook on low for about 6-8 hours, until chicken is tender and thoroughly cooked.
2. After which you can leave the lid off the crockpot.
3. Then you cook it on high for the last 30-45 minutes to thicken if you'd like, or mix 4 tablespoons cornstarch with ½ cup water and add that; cook 20-30 minutes longer on low.
4. However, this can also be made with chicken breasts; cook on low for about 4-6 hours until the chicken is done.

Saucy Crockpot Beef

Plant Paradox slow cooker cookbook

Tip:

1. Make sure you serve this rich and delicious savory Saucy Crockpot Beef recipe with a creamy sauce over hot mashed potatoes or hot cooked rice.
2. The last time I made this, I added a chopped onion and some minced garlic.

Ingredients

2 (10 ounce) can condensed cheddar cheese soup

4 pounds' beef stew meat (OR better still sirloin steak, cut into 1" cubes)

4 (10 ounce) cans condensed tomato soup

Preparation

1. First, you place meat in the crock pot and then pour the soups over the meat and mix well to combine.
2. After which you cover slow cooker and cook for 8 to 10 hrs. until meat is tender.
3. Then you stir well and serve over hot cooked rice or noodles.

Savory Crockpot Short Ribs

Ingredients

1 teaspoon of pepper

2 cups of barbecue sauce

1 teaspoon of dried thyme

1 teaspoon of paprika

8 lbs. of beef short ribs

24 oz. of jar beef gravy

2 lb. of frozen bell peppers and onions (thawed and drained)

1 teaspoon of dried basil

Preparation

1. First, you place in 3-4-quart crockpot ribs and sprinkle with pepper.
2. After which you mix in medium bowl, gravy and barbecue sauce and pour over top.
3. After that, you cover crockpot and cook on low for about 9-11 hours until beef is tender.
4. This is when you skim fat from surface of liquid in crockpot.
5. Then you add bell peppers, onions, herbs, and paprika to slow cooker and cover and cook on high 40-50 minutes until hot.
6. Finally, you serve vegetables and sauce with ribs.

Crockpot Poached Salmon

Tip:

1. Make sure you cook salmon to tender, moist perfection in your crockpot or slow cooker.
2. However, you should vary the seasonings according to your own tastes if you'd like.

Ingredients

4 tablespoons of lemon juice

1 teaspoon of salt

8 cloves garlic (minced)

1 teaspoon of dried dill weed

8 salmon steaks

2 cups of water

¼ teaspoon of white pepper

2 onion (sliced)

4 tablespoons of butter

Preparation

1. First, you grease the bottom of a 3-4 quart slow cooker and stack the salmon fillets in the appliance.
2. After which you combine remaining ingredients in a heavy saucepan and bring to a boil over high heat.
3. After that, you stir, then pour over salmon in crockpot.
4. Then you cover and cook on low for about 3-1/2 hours or until salmon flakes when tested with a fork.

Slow Cooker Momma's Roadhouse Chili

NUTRITIONAL INFORMATION

Serving Size: 1 cup.

Calories: 272

Total Fat: 7 gm

Sodium: 183 mg

Carbohydrates: 36 gm

Dietary Fiber: 13 gm

Sugars: 6 gm

Protein: 19 gm

Ingredients

2 small sweet onion

2 (15 ounces each) can black beans (drain)

2 (6 ounces each) can tomato paste

1 teaspoon of black pepper

1 teaspoon of crushed red pepper flakes

6 cups of water (for a thicker chili, I suggest you use 5 cups)

2-pound lean ground turkey, about 93% lean (it is optional, lean ground chicken or beef)

4 can (30 ounce) can kidney beans, drain

Plant Paradox slow cooker cookbook

2 (14.5 ounce each) diced tomatoes

5 tablespoons of chili powder

2 teaspoons of Kosher or sea salt

2 cups of tomato juice (or better still veggie juice)

Directions

1. First, you cook turkey and onion in a skillet on medium heat, breaking up into small chunks.
2. After which you cook until no longer pink.
3. After that, you drain off fat and discard.
4. Then you add cooked meat and all other ingredients to slow cooker.
5. Furthermore, you cook on low for 6-8 hours.
6. I recommend you use 4-6 quart slow cooker.
7. Finally, you add diced onions and cheddar cheese, if desired.

Slow Cooker Thai Curry Ground Beef
NUTRITIONAL INFORMATION

Serving Size: ¼ recipe.

Calories: 223.2

Fat: 8.7g

Carbs: 8g

Fiber: 1.6g

Protein: 25.2g

Ingredients

2 medium leek (sliced thin)

2 teaspoons of minced ginger

1 ½ cups of tomato sauce

2 tablespoons of soy sauce (make sure you use gluten free for Paleo and Gluten Free diets)

4 teaspoons of lime juice

2 lb. ground beef (93% lean)

4 garlic cloves (minced)

2 teaspoons – 2 tablespoons of red curry paste

2 teaspoons of lime zest

1 cup of light coconut milk

Directions:

Option 1:

1. First, you brown the ground beef and then add to the crockpot with the red curry paste, leek, garlic, ginger, tomato sauce, soy sauce, lime zest.
2. After which you cook on low for about 4 hours.
3. After that, you open the lid and stir in the coconut milk and lime juice.
4. Then you let cook for about 15 minutes longer and serve.

Option 2:

1. First, you heat a skillet over medium heat and spray with cooking spray.
2. After which you add the leeks and cook for about 4 minutes.
3. After that, you add the beef, garlic, and ginger and cook until beef is no longer pink.
4. Then you stir in the curry paste and cook for 1 minute.
5. Furthermore, you add the tomato sauce, lime zest, and soy sauce.
6. At this point, you turn the heat down to low and simmer for about 10 minutes.
7. Finally, you stir in the coconut milk and lime juice.
8. Then you let cook for 2 more minutes.

Slow Cooker Apple Cinnamon Oatmeal

NUTRITIONAL INFORMATION

Serving Size: 1 cup.

Calories: 205

Fat: 3g

Carbs: 38g

Protein: 7g

Ingredients

1 teaspoon of ground cinnamon

Pinches of salt

Enough water to fill Slow Cooker about ½ of the way full

Unrefined sweetener of choice (to taste)

1 cup of old fashioned (not quick cooking) oats

1 teaspoon of vanilla extract

4 cups of water

1 small apple (chopped)

Directions

1. First, you stir together in a small heat-proof bowl (that can hold at least four cups of water), the oats, cinnamon, vanilla, and salt. (Note: the apples can also be added in here).
2. As for me, I prefer to keep mine out to stir in after cooking, but this is up to you.

3. After that, you pour four cups water over oats.
4. Then you fill Slow Cooker about 1/4 to 1/2 of the way full with water (this will depend on the size of your Slow Cooker).
5. Furthermore, you add the heatproof bowl with the oat mixture to the Slow Cooker.
6. However, the bowl with the oats/cinnamon/vanilla has water in it, and also sits in the slow cooker surrounded by water.
7. Remember that the water level should rise almost to the top of the bowl.
8. At this point, you turn Slow Cooker on low for about 7-8 hours overnight.
9. In addition, you use a large spoon, remove bowl from Slow Cooker (note: it will be very hot!).
10. Finally, you stir in chopped apple and sweetener of choice.

Slow Cooker Balsamic Chicken

NUTRITIONAL INFORMATION

Serving Size: 1 cup.

Calories: 190

Fat: 6g

Carbs: 5g

Fiber: 1g

Protein: 26g

Ingredients

2 (14.5 oz.) can diced tomatoes

4 garlic cloves

1 tablespoon of olive oil

Ground black pepper and salt (to taste)

4-6 boneless, skinless, chicken breasts (about 40 ounces)

1 medium onion thinly sliced (NOTE: Not chopped)

½ cup of balsamic vinegar (for gluten-free, I suggest you use White Balsamic Vinegar which doesn't have caramel coloring)

1 teaspoon of each: dried oregano, basil, and rosemary

½ teaspoon of thyme

Plant Paradox slow cooker cookbook

Directions

1. First, you pour the olive oil on bottom of slow cooker.
2. After which you add chicken breasts, salt and pepper each breast, put sliced onion on top of chicken then put in all the dried herbs and garlic cloves.
3. After that, you pour in vinegar and top with tomatoes.
4. Then you cook on high for 4 hours, serve over angel hair pasta.

Slow Cooker Balsamic Chicken Wrap

Ingredients

2 tablespoons of prepared pesto (with no sugar added)

Leftover pieces of Balsamic Chicken

2 tomato and herb wrap

2 handful of baby spinach leaves

Directions

1. First, you place wrap on plate, spread with prepared pesto.
2. After which you add spinach leaves and top with chicken.
3. Then you wrap, slice in half and enjoy.

Slow Cooker Bananas Foster

NUTRITIONAL INFORMATION

Serving Size: ½ cup.

Calories: 110

Fat: 2 g

Carbohydrates: 28 g

Dietary fiber: 2 g

Protein: 2 g

Ingredients

6 tablespoons of honey

½ teaspoon of cinnamon

2 tablespoons of coconut oil, melted (unrefined coconut oil)

Juice from 1 lemon

1 teaspoon of 100% Rum Extract (it is optional)

10 bananas, medium firmness, 1/2" slices

Directions

1. First, you add and combine the first four ingredients to the slow cooker.
2. After which you add banana slices, toss gently to coat with honey mixture.
3. After that, you cover and cook on low for about 1 ½ to 2 hours.

4. Then you add rum extract to bananas and stir to combine.

Directions if you using Stovetop Method:

1. First, you combine the first 4 ingredients in a medium saucepan.
2. After which you add banana slices, toss gently to coat with honey mixture, cover and cook on low heat for approximately 30 minutes, or until heated through and bananas are soft but not falling apart.
3. After that, you add rum extract and stir to combine.
4. Then you can enjoy alone or over favorite desserts.

Slow Cooker Beef Stew

NUTRITIONAL INFORMATION

Calories: 263

Total Fat: 7 g

Sodium: 213 mg

Carbohydrates: 22 g

Dietary fiber: 4 g

Sugars: 5 g

Protein: 20 g

Ingredients

2 tablespoons of olive oil (remember flavored oil is wonderful to use: rosemary, basil, or Garlic-Chile pepper)

1 large white onion (chopped)

2 cups of potatoes (cut into 3/4 inch chunks)

2 carrots (peeled and chopped)

3 bay leaves

1 (about 14.5 ounce) can diced tomatoes

1-pound round steak (in 1 inch pieces)

Kosher or sea salt and pepper (to taste)

4 teaspoons of minced garlic

4 celery sticks (cleaned and chopped)

1 ½ teaspoons of dried thyme (or better still 1 tablespoon fresh thyme)

2 cups of beef broth (low sodium, fat free)

1 cup of red wine (it is optional, non-alcoholic wine or grape juice)

Directions

1. First, you rub the meat with oil, salt and pepper.
2. After which you let it sit at room temperature while preparing the other vegetables.
3. After that, you prepare all vegetables and add them to the slow cooker.
4. At this point, you place round steak on top of veggies.
5. Then you add the broth, wine, bay leaves, tomatoes, thyme, and a little salt and pepper.
6. Finally, you cover the slow cooker and cook on low for 8 hours, or until the meat is fork tender. I recommend you use a 4-6 quart slow cooker.

Slow Cooker Butter Chicken

NUTRITIONAL INFORMATION

Serving Size: ¾ cup.

Calories: 240.1

Fat: 13.8g

Carbs: 5.1g

Fiber: 7g

Protein: 24.7g

Ingredients

2 tablespoons of vegetable oil

½ white onion (chopped)

4 teaspoons of lemon juice

2-inch ginger (minced)

2 teaspoons of chili powder

2 bay leaves

½ cup of half and half

2 cups of tomato sauce

2 pinches of black pepper

4 lbs. of chicken breast (cubed)

2 shallots (finely chopped)

4 tablespoons of butter

8 garlic cloves (minced)

4 teaspoons of garam masala

2 teaspoons of ground cumin

½ cup of plain nonfat yogurt

1 ½ cups of skim milk

4 ½ teaspoons of cayenne pepper (or to taste)

2 pinches of salt

Directions:

1. First, you heat the oil in a medium sauce pan, over medium heat.
2. After which you add the shallot and onion and sauté until soft.
3. After that, you add the ginger, garlic, butter, lemon juice, garam masala, cayenne, chili powder, cumin, and bay leaf and cook for 1 minute until fragrant.
4. Then you add the tomato sauce and cook for 2 minutes stirring often.
5. In addition, you add the half and half, milk, and yogurt.
6. After which you reduce heat to low, stir, and simmer for about 10 minutes.
7. At this point, you stir frequently.
8. This is when you take a taste and season with salt and pepper.
9. Furthermore, you add everything to a blender and blend until well combined.
10. Finally, you add cubed chicken breast to the slow cooker and cook for 4 hours.
11. You can enjoy it better with rice or cauliflower rice.

Crockpot Black Bean Chili Recipe

TIPs:
This recipe is a healthy and delicious vegetarian chili recipe made with black beans and lots of veggies cooks in your slow cooker (it obvious that any chili recipe really combines already cooked ingredients). Cooking blends together and enhances the individual flavors of this recipe.

Ingredients

2 large onions (diced)

1 red bell pepper (chopped)

3 (14 oz.) cans diced tomatoes (undrained)

1 Tablespoon of chili powder

10 oz. of pkg. frozen corn

1 cup of picante (or better still taco sauce)

2 Tablespoons of olive oil

3 cloves garlic (minced)

1 green bell pepper (chopped)

2 teaspoons of cumin

½ teaspoon of crushed red pepper flakes

2 (15 oz.) cans black beans (drained and rinsed)

Preparation

1. First, you sauté in a heavy skillet the onions in the olive oil until tender, stirring frequently.
2. After which you add garlic and cook for 2 minutes longer.
3. After that, you add cumin and cayenne pepper, and other spices you might like.
4. Then you cook for two minutes longer.
5. At this point, you mix all ingredients into a 4-5 quart slow cooker.
6. Finally, you cover and cook on low for about 10 hours (NOTE: If you have a newer, hotter cooking crockpot, I suggest you cook on low for 6-7 hours).

Crockpot BBQ Pinto Beans

Tips:

This simple and flavorful recipe is perfect as a side dish for a juicy grilled steak.

Ingredients

6 cups of water

36 oz. bottle barbecue sauce

½ teaspoon of pepper

2 lb. of dried pinto beans

2 onions (chopped)

½ cup of molasses or honey

Preparation

1. First, you sort beans, rinse and drain.
2. After which you cover with water and let stand, covered, overnight.
3. After that, the next morning, you drain the beans again and rinse them.
4. Then you combine beans, 6 cups water, onion, barbecue sauce, molasses, and pepper in 4-quart crockpot.
5. Finally, you cover crockpot and cook on low for about 8-9 hours or until beans are tender.

NOTE: if you have a newer crockpot that cooks hotter, I suggest you check at 7 hours and stir the beans once at the halfway point.

NUTRITIONAL INFORMATION

Calories: 370
Fat: 5 grams
Sodium: 840 mg

Crockpot Black and White Fondue

Tips:

1. This recipe is not only delicious but beautiful too.
2. Make sure you use the freshest fruit possible for dippers.

Ingredients

36 oz. semisweet chocolate (chopped)

2 tablespoons of Grand Marnier (if desired)

Cookies, pound cake squares, brownies, strawberries, blackberries, apples, pears

4 oz. unsweetened baking chocolate (chopped)

28 oz. can sweetened condensed milk

2 teaspoons of vanilla

8 oz. white chocolate (finely chopped)

Preparation

1. First, you combine in 2-quart crockpot (Crockett), baking chocolate, semisweet chocolate, and sweetened condensed milk and mix well.
2. After which you cover and cook on LOW for about 1 hour until chocolate is melted.
3. After that, you stir well, then add Grand Marnier, if using, and vanilla.
4. Mix well.

5. Then you sprinkle white chocolate over the melted chocolate mixture, cover, and cook for 10-12 minutes on LOW until white chocolate is melted.
6. Finally, you stir gently to marble, then serve.

Crockpot Apricot Pork Sandwiches

Tip:

1. Dried apricots and apricot preserves add wonderful flavor to this easy Crockpot Apricot Pulled Pork Sandwiches recipe.

Ingredients

About 16 oz. of jar apricot preserves

2 cloves garlic (minced)

1 cup of canned condensed French onion soup

1 onion (chopped)

Baby spinach leaves

3 lb. of boneless pork shoulder roast

1/3 cup of finely chopped dried apricots

Salt and pepper to taste

2 Tablespoons of Dijon mustard

Toasted Kaiser Rolls

Preparation

1. First, you trim roast of excess fat.
2. After which you place roast in 4-6-quart crockpot.

3. After that, you mix preserves, apricots, garlic, salt, and pepper, onion soup, mustard and onion in a small bowl, then pour over meat in crockpot.
4. Then you cover and cook on low heat setting for about 7-9 hours.
5. At this point, you remove meat from crockpot, let stand for about 5-10 minutes, then shred meat with a fork.
6. This is when you skim the fat off liquid remaining in crockpot.
7. Furthermore, you return pork to crockpot and stir well.
8. Finally, you make sandwiches using meat mixture, rolls, and baby spinach leaves.

Crockpot Cajun Pot Roast

TIPS:

1. If you can't find Cajun Seasoning in your area, I suggest you make Creole Meat Seasoning and keep on hand for this recipe and many more.

Ingredients

2 tablespoons of Cajun seasoning

24 oz. of can diced tomatoes with garlic (undrained)

¼ teaspoon of pepper

4lb. of boneless beef chuck roast

2 onion (chopped)

1 teaspoon of Tabasco sauce

Preparation

1. First, you sprinkle Cajun seasoning over roast and rub to coat well.
2. After which you place in 4-6-quart crockpot and top with onion.
3. After that, you combine the tomatoes with their juice, hot pepper sauce and pepper in small bowl.
4. Then you pour over vegetables and roast.
5. Finally, you cover and cook on low setting for about 8-10 hours.

Crockpot Caribbean Ribs

Ingredients

2 teaspoons of pepper

2 teaspoons of ground mustard

3 cups of barbecue sauce

6 pounds' pork loin back ribs (cut into 4" pieces)

1 teaspoon of allspice

2 teaspoons of salt

1 cup of water

Preparation

1. First, you combine all spices in a small bowl.
2. After which you rub ribs with spice mixture.
3. After that, you place in 3-4 quart slow cooker and pour water over.
4. Then you cover and cook on low for about 8-9 hours or until ribs are tender when pierced with a fork.
5. At this point, you remove ribs from slow cooker and discard cooking liquid.
6. This is when you replace ribs in crockpot and add barbecue sauce.
7. Finally, you cover and cook on low for 1 hour.

NUTRITIONAL INFORMATION

Serving size: per serving

Plant Paradox slow cooker cookbook

Calories: 330
Fat: 19 grams
Sodium: 1500 mg

Crockpot Chicken Alfredo

Tips:

1. This easy and nutritious recipe combines chicken thighs with lots of vegetables and Alfredo sauce.

Ingredients

2 onions (chopped)

1 red bell pepper (chopped)

4 cups of frozen broccoli florets

¼ cup of grated Parmesan cheese

2 lbs. of boneless, skinless chicken thighs, cubed

4 cloves garlic (minced)

About 16-oz. jar four cheese Alfredo sauce

About 9-oz. pkg. refrigerated fettuccine

Preparation

1. First, you place chicken, onions, garlic, and red bell pepper in 4-quart crockpot.
2. After which you pour Alfredo sauce over.
3. After that, you cover crockpot and cook on low for about 7-8 hours.
4. Then you thaw and drain broccoli and add to crockpot along with fettuccine.

5. At this point you stir well, cover crockpot, and cook on high for about 30-40 minutes, until broccoli is hot and fettuccine is tender.
6. Finally, you sprinkle with cheese and serve.

Crockpot Chicken and Apples

Ingredients

¼ teaspoon of ground nutmeg

4 tablespoons of butter

4 garlic cloves (minced)

Salt and pepper (to taste)

4 tablespoons of apple cider vinegar

2 tablespoons of cornstarch

2 cups of apple cider

2 tablespoons of curry powder

2 onions (chopped)

12 boneless, skinless chicken breasts

6 Granny Smith apples (cored and thickly sliced)

2/3 cup chicken broth

Preparation

1. First, you combine in small bowl the apple cider, nutmeg, and curry powder.
2. After which you combine butter, onions, and garlic in a small microwave-safe dish.
3. After that, you microwave on high for about 1-2 minutes until onion is softened.

4. At this point, you place mixture in bottom of 3-4 quart slow cooker.
5. This is when you dip each chicken breast into the juice mixture to coat and place in crockpot over onions.
6. Then you pour any remaining juice mixture over the chicken
7. Furthermore, you add salt and pepper to taste.
8. After that, you cover and cook on low for about 5-6 hours until chicken is almost cooked.
9. Then you add apples and cook for about 40-50 minutes longer on low until apples are tender and chicken is thoroughly cooked.
10. In addition, you mix vinegar, broth and cornstarch in a small bowl and stir into the liquid in crockpot.
11. After which you cover and cook on high heat, stirring occasionally, until sauce is thickened and bubbly, about 10-15 minutes.
12. Finally, you serve with some hot cooked brown rice.

NOTE:

Remember, if you have a new hot crockpot, check the chicken after 4 hours on low.

If the sauce does not get thick enough, I suggest you add more cornstarch mixed with chicken broth or apple cider vinegar.

Crockpot Cheesy Potatoes

Tips:

1. This recipe uses frozen hash brown potatoes in a wonderful four ingredient recipe.
2. Remember that this crockpot Cheesy Potatoes is perfect for entertaining and for busy days during the holidays.

Ingredients

About 8 oz. container sour cream

About 32 oz. pkg. of frozen hash brown potatoes

About 10 oz. of can condensed cream of mushroom soup

1-1/2 cups of shredded Carjack cheese

Preparation

1. First, you spray 4-6 quart slow cooker with cooking spray.
2. After which you combine soup, sour cream and cheese in medium bowl and mix well.
3. After that, you pour half of potatoes into prepared crockpot.
4. Then you top with half of sour cream mixture.
5. Furthermore, you top with rest of potatoes, then remaining sour cream mixture, spreading evenly.
6. Finally, you cover and cook on high for about 3-1/2 to 4-1/2 hours.

NOTE: If you have a newer, hotter crockpot, I suggest you check at 3 hours to see if the potatoes are tender.

NUTRITIONAL INFORMATION

Serving Size: per serving

Calories: 200
Fat: 10 grams
Sodium: 270 mg

Crockpot Chicken and Shrimp

Tips:
This recipe is fancy enough for company.

Ingredients

1 teaspoon of salt

½ teaspoon of crushed red pepper flakes

8 cloves garlic (minced)

6 tablespoons of tomato paste

2 teaspoons of dried thyme leaves

6 tablespoons of lemon juice

24 ounces can of artichoke hearts (drained and chopped)

1 1/3 cup of crumbled feta cheese

2 pound boneless, skinless chicken thighs

¼ teaspoon of pepper

4 onions (chopped)

28 ounces can of seasoned diced tomatoes

2 cups of chicken broth

1 teaspoon of dried basil leaves

16-ounce package frozen cooked shrimp, thawed

2 tablespoon cornstarch

Preparation

1. First, you cut chicken into large chunks and sprinkle with salt and pepper to taste.
2. After which you place onion and garlic in bottom of a 3-4 quart slow cooker and top with chicken.
3. After that, you combine the diced tomatoes with their liquid, the tomato paste, chicken broth, thyme, basil, and lemon juice in a medium bowl and mix well.
4. Then you pour over chicken.
5. At this point, you cover crockpot and cook on low for 6-8 hours until chicken is tender and thoroughly cooked.
6. Furthermore, you stir in thawed and drained shrimp, thawed, and drained and chopped artichoke hearts mixed with cornstarch.
7. After which you cover and cook for about 15-20 minutes longer until thoroughly heated and slightly thickened.
8. Finally, you serve over hot cooked pasta or couscous and sprinkle with feta cheese.

Plant Paradox slow cooker cookbook

Crockpot Chicken Cacciatore

Tip:

This rich and delicious recipe is low in fat and sodium, and is made so easily in your slow cooker.

Ingredients

14 oz. of can diced tomatoes with Italian seasoning

1 cup of chicken broth

4 cloves garlic (minced)

1 cup of sliced mushrooms

1 teaspoon of dried Italian seasoning

½ teaspoon of salt

3 Tablespoons of water

3 lbs. bone-in chicken thighs or drumsticks (skin removed)

6 oz. can of tomato paste

1 onion (sliced)

1 green bell pepper (chopped)

½ cup of dry red wine

¼ teaspoon of pepper

2 tablespoons of cornstarch

Preparation

1. First, you place all ingredients except cornstarch and water in 4-5 quart slow cooker.
2. After which you cover and cook on low 6-8 hours until chicken is thoroughly cooked and tender.

NOTE: if you want a thicker sauce, I suggest you combine cornstarch and water in small bowl and mix well.

3. After that, you stir into crockpot; cover and cook on low for 15-20 minutes until thickened.
4. Finally, you serve with hot cooked pasta, if desired.

Crockpot Chicken Sweet Potatoes

Tip:

1. This wonderful and easy crockpot chicken sweet potatoes is so good for you! One serving supplies 100% of the Vitamin A you need every day. And it's delicious too.

Ingredients

2 teaspoons of salt

2 teaspoons of paprika

1 teaspoon of ground ginger

2 onions (chopped)

6 tablespoons of apple cider vinegar

4 tablespoons of cornstarch

16 boneless, skinless chicken thighs

¼ teaspoon of cayenne pepper

2 teaspoons of curry powder

6 sweet potatoes (peeled and cubed)

2 cups of peach preserves (OR better still apricot preserves)

2 tablespoons of low-sodium soy sauce

1 cup of chicken broth or water

Preparation

1. First, you sprinkle chicken with salt, paprika, cayenne pepper, curry powder, and ginger.
2. After which you place sweet potatoes and onions in 3-1/2 quart slow cooker and top with chicken.
3. After that, you top with peach preserves, vinegar, and soy sauce.
4. Then you cover and cook on low for about 6-8 hours until chicken is thoroughly cooked and sweet potatoes are tender when pierced with fork.
5. At this point, you combine chicken broth and cornstarch, mix well and add to slow cooker.
6. Finally, you cover and cook on high for about 10-15 minutes until sauce is thickened.

NUTRITIONAL INFORMATION

Serving Size: per serving
Calories: 380
Fat: 12 grams
Sodium: 700 mg

Crockpot Chicken Wild Rice Casserole

Tip:

1. This delicious and homey one-dish meal is rich, easy and you will love how the wild rice cooks in the crockpot, absorbing the flavors of the other ingredients.

Ingredients

2 onions (chopped)

24 oz. can condensed chicken broth

20 oz. can condensed cream of chicken soup

2 ½ cups of wild rice

½ teaspoon of dried marjoram

12 slices of bacon

4 cloves garlic (minced)

2 2/3 cups of water

18 oz. bag baby carrots

3 lbs. boneless, skinless chicken breasts (cut into 1" pieces)

Preparation

1. First, you cook bacon in large skillet until crisp.
2. After which you remove bacon, crumble and refrigerate.
3. After that, you remove all but 2 tablespoon bacon drippings from skillet.

4. Then you add onion and garlic to skillet and cook and stir for about 2-3 minutes.
5. Furthermore, you stir in broth, water, and condensed soup.
6. Cook and stir for about 3-4 minutes until bubbly.
7. After that, you place wild rice and carrots in 3-4-quart crockpot.
8. This is when you top with chicken pieces and pour mixture in skillet over chicken.
9. Then you sprinkle with marjoram.
10. In addition, you cover crockpot and cook on high for about 1 hour.
11. After which you stir mixture, making sure wild rice is submerged in liquid.
12. At this point, you reduce crockpot setting to low and cook, covered, for 6-8 hours until chicken is thoroughly cooked and wild rice is tender.
13. Finally, you sprinkle reserved bacon into crockpot during the last 30 minutes of cooking time.
14. Then you stir gently and serve.

Crockpot Chicken Chili

Ingredients

3 (14 oz.) cans diced tomatoes with chilies and garlic (undrained)

2 (15 oz.) cans white beans (drained and rinsed)

2 lbs. of boneless, skinless chicken thighs

1 oz. pkg. taco seasoning mix OR 2 tablespoons of Homemade Taco Seasoning Mix

3 cups of water

Preparation

1. First, you combine all ingredients in a 4-5-quart crockpot.
2. After which you cover and cook on low for about 7-9 hours or until chicken is tender and no longer pink.
3. Then you stir well so the chicken breaks into small pieces.

NUTRITIONAL INFORMATION

Serving Size: per serving

Calories: 400
Fat: 14 grams
Sodium: 1600 mg

Crockpot Chicken Chowder Recipe

Tip:

1. Feel free to make this delicious creamy low fat Crockpot Chicken Chowder for dinner tonight.
2. Dried potatoes flakes (which are made from real potatoes) are a great way to thicken soups and stews without adding any fat or sodium.

Ingredients

2 cups of skim milk

¼ teaspoon of white pepper

4 cloves garlic (minced)

2 lbs. boneless, skinless chicken breasts (cut into 1" pieces)

1 cup of grated Parmesan cheese

2 cups of chopped carrots

4 cups of low sodium chicken broth

2 onions (chopped)

2 potatoes (peeled and cubed)

4 (30 oz.) cans creamed corn

½ cup of dried potato flakes

Preparation

1. First, you combine all ingredients except dried potato flakes and cheese in slow cooker.

2. After which you cover and cook on low for about 5-6 hours or until potatoes are tender and chicken thoroughly cooked.
3. After that, you add potato flakes and stir well to combine.
4. Then you cook mixture on high, uncovered, for about 5-10 minutes or until chowder has thickened and dried potato flakes have dissolved.
5. Finally, you top each serving with cheese.

NUTRITIONAL INFORMATION

Serving Size: per serving

Calories: 385
Fat: 4.8 grams
Carbs: 65 grams
Sodium: 1065 mg
Cholesterol: 42 mg
Vitamin A: 85% DV

Slow Cooker Cranberry Sauce

NUTRITIONAL INFORMATION

Serving Size: 2 tbsp.

Calories: 73

Fat: 0g

Sodium: 1 mg

Carbohydrate: 19 g

Fiber: 2 g

Sugar: 16 g

Protein: 0 g

Ingredients

1 cup of fresh squeezed orange juice (with no sugar added)

1 cup of honey

2 (about 24 oz.) bag fresh cranberries

2 large cinnamon stick

Directions

1. First, you combine all ingredients in slow cooker.
2. After which you cook for 5-6 hours on low, or until berries are soft.
3. After that, you remove the lid and continue to cook for 1-2 hours on high so the liquids can cook down.
4. Then you chill in the fridge overnight or until set.

Slow Cooker Hearty Vegetable and Bean Soup

NUTRITIONAL INFORMATION

Serving Size: 1 ½ cup.

Calories: 183

Fat: 4 g

Sodium: 253 mg

Carbohydrates: 17 g

Dietary Fiber: 4 g

Sugars: 5 g

Protein: 6 g

Ingredients

4 cloves garlic (minced)

4 carrots (peeled and sliced into 1" pieces)

2 cups of whole kernel corn (It is optional)

1 teaspoon of black pepper

2 teaspoons of paprika

1 teaspoon of crushed red pepper flakes, more or less to taste (it can be substituted with cayenne pepper)

8 cups of vegetable broth, low sodium (remember, chicken broth can be substituted)

2 (29 oz.) can diced tomatoes

2 sweet onion (diced)

2 media sweet potato, peeled and cut into 1" cubes (it is optional, white or red potato)

4 stalks celery (diced)

Kosher or sea salt (to taste)

¼ teaspoon of allspice

2 bay leaves

4 cups of frozen (or preferably fresh green beans)

½ cup of freshly chopped parsley

4 cans cannellini beans, drained and rinsed (preferably navy, black, pinto or chick peas can be substituted)

Directions

1. First, you add all the above ingredients to the slow cooker.
2. After which you stir to combine, cover and cook on low for 8-10 hours or until carrots are tender.

Note: if you want to make this a meat dish, I suggest you add 2-pound chicken fillets (cut into 1" cubes) to slow cooker along with the other ingredients.

Tip:

1. If you want a thicker soup, near the end of cooking time, I suggest you remove 1 cup of soup (liquid and veggies) and combine with 2-4 tablespoons of flour or corn starch.
2. After which you puree and return to the slow cooker.
3. Remember a fork works well to mash the ingredients along with the flour or cornstarch.

4. However, be careful not to allow the hot mixture to spin out.
5. You should continue cooking for about 15 minutes until soup thickens.

Slow Cooker Honey Bananas

Minimum Slow Cooker Size: 2 quarts

NUTRITIONAL INFORMATION

Serving Size: ½ cup.

Calories: 109

Fat: 1 gm

Sodium: 1 mg

Carbohydrates: 27 gm

Dietary fiber: 2 gm

Sugars: 18 gm

Protein: 1 gm

Ingredients

2 tablespoons of coconut oil

Juice from 1 lemon

Chopped hazelnuts or preferably almonds for sprinkling (it is optional)

8 bananas

6 tablespoon of raw honey

1 teaspoon of crushed Cardamom Seeds

Directions

1. First, you put coconut oil in slow cooker, turn on and melt if needed.
2. After which you peel bananas and cut diagonally in 1/2" slices.
3. After that, you place bananas in the slow cooker.
4. At this point, you sprinkle lemon juice and cardamom over bananas.
5. Then you add honey and stir to ensure bananas well coated without breaking.
6. This is when you cook on low for about 2 hours.
7. Finally, you sprinkle with nuts if desired.
8. Enjoy!

Slow Cooker Herb Chicken and Vegetables

NUTRITIONAL INFORMATION

Serving Size: 1/6 of recipe.

Calories: 207

Fat: 10 g

Sodium: 22 mg

Carbohydrates: 23 g

Dietary fiber: 3 g

Sugars: 3 g

Protein: 7 g

Ingredients

One parsnip (peeled, sliced into 1/4" round pieces)

3 garlic cloves (minced)

3 bone-in, split chicken breast (skinless)

One teaspoon of paprika

Kosher or sea salt (to taste)

2 tablespoons of fresh parsley, (2 teaspoons dried parsley (it is optional)

One tablespoon of fresh rosemary, (1 teaspoon dried rosemary (it is optional)

Plant Paradox slow cooker cookbook

One carrot (peeled, sliced into 1/4" round pieces)

One pound small red potatoes (about 6 baby potatoes, quartered and cut into small wedges)

One yellow onion (quartered and cut into small wedges)

¼ cup of extra-virgin olive oil

½ teaspoon of black pepper

One tablespoon of fresh sage, (1 teaspoon dried rubbed sage (it is optional)

1 tablespoon fresh thyme, (1 teaspoon dried thyme (it is optional)

Directions

1. First, you add parsnips, carrots, potatoes onion and garlic to a medium mixing bowl.
2. After which you combine in a small bowl, the oil, paprika, herbs, salt and pepper.
3. After that, you add half oil and herb mixture to vegetables, toss to coat and add to slow cooker.
4. At this point, you rinse and pat chicken dry.
5. Add to the mixing bowl and pour remaining oil and herb mixture over chicken, being sure to thoroughly coat.
6. Then in a large skillet, you turn to medium-high heat, add chicken and lightly brown on both sides.
7. Finally, you place chicken over vegetables, cover and cook on low for about 5-6 hours or until juices run clear when pierced with a fork, or chicken has reached an internal temperature of 165 degrees and vegetables are tender.

Slow Cooker Hot Chocolate Steel-Cut Oatmeal

NUTRITIONAL INFORMATION

Serving Size: 1 cup.

Calories: 126

Fat: 8 g

Sodium: 160 mg

Carbohydrates: 12.4 g

Dietary Fiber: 2.1 g

Sugars: 4.4 g

Protein: 2.7 g

Ingredients

8 cups of water

2 tablespoons of cocoa powder

½ teaspoon of salt

16 drops of liquid stevia (or preferably an extra tablespoon of sugar)

2 cups of steel-cut oats

1 cup of coconut milk

2 teaspoons of vanilla

2 tablespoons of coconut palm sugar (or better still pure maple syrup)

Directions

1. First, you combine in a large bowl the water, milk, vanilla, and stevia.
2. After which you whisk in the cocoa, sugar, and salt.
3. After that, you stir in the oats.
4. Furthermore, you oil the inside of your slow cooker (this prevents the oatmeal from sticking).
5. At this point, you pour in the above mixture.
6. Then you set your slow cooker too low for about 1-2 hours, and turn it to KEEP WARM before finally retiring to bed.
7. Finally, in the morning you give it all a stir and feast! And then top with some shaved chocolate if you're feeling really decadent!

Slow Cooker Home-style Potatoes with Garlic and Rosemary

NUTRITIONAL INFORMATION

Calories: 179

Fat: 9 g

Sodium: 6 mg

Carbohydrates: 23 g

Dietary Fiber: 2 g

Sugars: 1 g

Protein: 2 g

Ingredients

8 medium red potatoes, cubed into 1/2" pieces (unpeeled if desired)

2 tablespoons of chopped fresh rosemary

Kosher or sea salt (to taste)

½ cup of extra virgin olive oil (NOTE: evoo is a good fat)

6 cloves garlic (minced)

1 teaspoon of black pepper

Directions

1. First, you add oil to the slow cooker, turn to high and allow to heat up while preparing potatoes…about 15 minutes of preheating is good.
2. After which you combine all ingredients in the slow cooker.
3. After that, you toss potatoes in oil, cover and cook on high for 2-3 hours (4-5 hours on low), or until potatoes are tender and browned.
4. Remember that fats in this recipe are from heart healthy extra-virgin olive oil.

Crockpot Italian Beef

NUTRITIONAL INFORMATION

Serving Size: about ½ cup.

Calories: 198.7

Fat: 8.4g

Carbs: 1.8g

Fiber: 2g

Protein: 24.8g

Ingredients

1 onion (sliced)

1 tablespoon of dried Italian seasoning

½ cup of red wine

Salt and pepper to taste

2 lb. of boneless beef brisket (trimmed of all fat)

4-6 cloves garlic (minced)

1 teaspoon of red pepper flakes

2 cups of fat free beef broth

Directions:

1. First, you season the beef with salt and pepper.
2. After which you add everything to the slow cooker.
3. After that, you cook on low for about 8 hours until beef shreds easily with fork.
4. However, if you will be using the beef in Italian beef sandwiches, you can strain the broth to make an au jus for dipping (I highly recommend you taking this step).

Slow Cooker Lentil & Veggie Stew

NUTRITIONAL INFORMATION

Serving Size: 1 ½ cup.

Calories: 221

Fat: 2 g

Sodium: 312 mg

Carbohydrates: 42 g

Dietary fiber: 11 g

Sugars: 7 g

Protein: 11 g

Ingredients

1 large red potato (cut into 1" cubes)

½ cup of diced sweet onion

1 cup of (fresh or better still frozen) green beans (broken into 1" pieces)

½ teaspoon of black pepper

1 ½ cups of tomato juice, low sodium (V-8 Juice low-sodium (optional)

1 cup of (dry) lentils

1 cup of frozen or better still fresh whole kernel corn

Plant Paradox slow cooker cookbook

4 carrots (sliced)

2 stalks celery (sliced into 1/2" pieces)

½ teaspoon of paprika

Kosher or sea salt (to taste)

3 cups of vegetable broth, low sodium (chicken broth (optional)

Directions

1. First, you add all of the above ingredients, except lentils, to the slow cooker.
2. After which you stir to combine.
3. After that, you cover and cook on low for 8 to 10 hours.
4. Then you add lentils the last hour of cooking time.
5. You can add or substitute your favorite vegetables.

Tip:

1. Feel free to adjust the liquid for less or more thickness.
2. Try adding 1 cup each tomato juice and 1 cup vegetable broth.
3. However, the slow cooker does not give room for much evaporation, so the amount of liquid you add initially will be about the same toward the end of the cooking cycle.
4. Remember it is easier to add liquid than to remove it.

I recommend you use a minimum slow cooker size 4 quarts.

Slow Cooker Paprika Pork Tenderloin
NUTRITIONAL INFORMATION

Serving Size: 4 oz.

Calories: 160.1

Fat: 8.2g

Carbs: 2.4g

Fiber: 3g

Protein: 21.7g

Ingredients

2 cups of chicken stock

4 tablespoons of smoked paprika

Black pepper

3 lb. of pork tenderloin

1 cup of your favorite salsa

2 tablespoons of oregano

1 teaspoon of salt

Directions:

1. First, you stir together in a small bowl the chicken stock, oregano, salsa, paprika, salt, and pepper.
2. After which you add the pork, trimmed of fat, to the slow cooker.

3. After that, you pour over the sauce and cook on high for about 4 hours.
4. Then you shred the pork with two forks and cook with the top off for an additional 20 minutes so all the juice is absorbed.

Slow Cooker Pomegranate Chicken Breasts

NUTRITIONAL INFORMATION

Serving Size: 1 breast.

Calories: 279

Fat: 10 g

Sodium: 225 mg

Carbohydrates: 19 g

Dietary fiber: 1 g

Sugars: 17 g

Protein: 26 g

Ingredients

1 teaspoon of black pepper

2 teaspoons of coriander

½ teaspoon of cayenne pepper

4 tablespoons of extra virgin olive oil

4 tablespoons of honey

2 tablespoons of white balsamic vinegar

8 chicken breasts, boneless, skinless (3 – 4lbs)

Kosher or sea salt (to taste)

2 teaspoons of chili powder

4 teaspoons of dried oregano

2 tablespoons of Dijon Mustard

4 garlic cloves (minced)

3 cups of pomegranate juice, (with no sugar added)

Directions

1. First, you combine all the herbs and spices in a small mixing bowl.
2. After which you whisk together in a large mixing bowl the herbs, spices and the extra virgin olive oil.
3. After that, you rinse chicken, pat dry with a paper towel.
4. At this point, you coat chicken with the herb and oil mixture, place in the slow-cooker.
5. Remember that this method of rubbing olive oil on the chicken before adding to the slow-cooker helps to seal in the moisture.
6. This is when you whisk together in a medium mixing bowl Dijon mustard, honey, minced garlic, pomegranate juice and balsamic vinegar...pour over chicken.
7. Furthermore, you turn slow cooker to low and cook for 4 - 6 hours on low.
8. Once the chicken is done remove from the slow cooker.
9. Then you place on a serving platter and drizzle with liquid (NOTE: This extra moist chicken pairs nicely with a small side of pasta).
10. If you are using the Set 'n Forget Slow Cooker, make sure you program the temperature to 165 degrees or follow manufacturer's instructions.

Slow Cooker Pork Avocado

NUTRITIONAL INFORMATION
Serving Size: about 6 ounces.

Calories: 165

Fat: 7g

Carbs: 4.1g

Fiber: 1g

Protein: 24.1g

Ingredients

3 ounces of dried New Mexico Chiles

6 garlic cloves

1 tablespoon of coriander

1 teaspoon of dried oregano

¼ cup of cilantro (for garnish)

3 lbs. of pork shoulder (trimmed of fat)

2 chipotles in adobo

1 onion (chopped into quarters)

1 teaspoon of cumin

2 bay leaves

Salt and pepper

Plant Paradox slow cooker cookbook

Directions:

1. First, you toast in a sauté pan the dried New Mexico chilies for about 3-5 minutes until fragrant and begin to puff up (NOTE: This brings out their full flavor).
2. Once they cool, you remove the seeds and stem.
3. After that, you add the chilies to small pot and cover with water.
4. Then you bring to a boil and then let simmer for about 5 minutes.
5. At this point, you turn off the heat and allow the chilies to rest in the water for about 30 minutes.
6. Furthermore, you add the Chile peppers and 1 cup of their cooking liquid, the chipotles, cumin, oregano, coriander, garlic, and onion to a blender and blend until combined (NOTE: This creates the adobo sauce).
7. After which you season the pork shoulder with salt and pepper.
8. After that, you pour a small amount of the adobo sauce into the bottom of the slow cooker.
9. This is when you place the pork shoulder on top and pour in the remaining adobo sauce.
10. Then you cook in your slow cooker for about 6-8 hours until the pork is fork tender.
11. In addition, you pull the pork apart using a fork and mix together with the sauce.
12. Finally, you serve on its own, over rice, win a sandwich for a spicy pulled pork, or in tacos.
13. Then you garnish with freshly chopped cilantro.

Slow Cooker Pork Roast with Vegetables

Tip:

This delicious recipe for Slow Cooker Pork Roast with Vegetables combines a sirloin roast with lots of veggies, seasoned to perfection with allspice and apple butter.

Ingredients

1 Tablespoon of vegetable oil

2 sweet potatoes (peeled)

3 Tablespoons of prepared horseradish

½ teaspoon of ground allspice

1 teaspoon of dried thyme leaves

3 lb. of boneless pork sirloin roast

1 acorn squash

½ cup of apple butter

1 Tablespoon of cornstarch

¼ teaspoon of pepper

1 cup of chicken broth

Preparation

1. First, you heat oil in a heavy skillet and cook pork roast until browned on all sides, turning occasionally (NOTE: This should take approximately 10 minutes).

2. Then while that's cooking, you cut the acorn squash into 8 wedges and remove seeds (NOTE: Do not peel).
3. Furthermore, you peel sweet potatoes and cut into chunks.
4. After which you place squash and sweet potatoes in 6-7 quart slow cooker.
5. After that, you top with browned pork roast.
6. At this point, you mix together in a small bowl the apple butter, allspice, pepper, horseradish, cornstarch, chicken broth, and thyme.
7. This is when you pour into slow cooker.
8. Finally, you cover crockpot and cook on low for about 7-9 hours until pork and vegetables are tender.

NUTRITIONAL INFORMATION

Calories: 410
Fat: 12 grams
Sodium: 200 mg

Slow Cooker Pork Tenderloin

NUTRITIONAL INFORMATION

Calories: 252

Fat: 0 g

Sodium: 816 mg

Carbohydrates: 15 g

Dietary Fiber: 0 g

Sugars: 13 g

Protein: 32 g

Ingredients

1 ½ - 2 pounds of lean pork tenderloin

Ingredients for the Marinade:

1 tablespoon of Dijon mustard

1 tablespoon of lite soy sauce, low sodium (Tamari or Bragg Liquid (optional)

2 teaspoons of freshly grated ginger

1 teaspoon of curry powder

Kosher or sea salt (to taste)

1 cup of chicken broth (fat-free, low-sodium)

1 tablespoon of rice wine vinegar

2 tablespoons honey

2 cloves garlic (minced)

½ teaspoon of black pepper

Glaze: (it is optional)

2 tablespoons of lite soy sauce (or better still try BRAGG Liquid Aminos)

2 tablespoons of ketchup

1 tablespoon of Dijon mustard

2 tablespoons of honey

2 tablespoons of rice wine vinegar

1 tablespoon of sesame oil

Directions

1. First, you combine in a large mixing bowl all marinade ingredients.
2. After which you trim away all visible fat from tenderloin and discard.
3. After that, you cut tenderloin into 2" pieces and place in marinade, ensuring all sides are coated.
4. Then you cover and allow tenderloin to marinate overnight in the refrigerator.
5. At this point, you place tenderloin and marinade in slow cooker, cook on low 4-6 hours, or until it shreds easily with a fork.

6. Finally, you remove from the slow cooker and place on a serving platter.

Directions on how to prepare glaze:

1. First, you add all ingredients to a small saucepan, bring to a boil, reduce heat to a simmer.
2. After that, you cook for about 5 minutes or until desired thickness.
3. Then you pour glaze over tenderloin.

Slow Cooker Salsa Chicken

NUTRITIONAL INFORMATION

Serving Size: 1 cup.

Calories: 432

Fat: 3.9 g

Sodium: 374 mg

Carbohydrates: 72.5 g

Dietary Fiber: 9.0 g

Sugars: 4.2 g

Protein: 27.2 g

Ingredients

1 small onion (diced)

1 lb. of boneless, skinless chicken breasts (cut into 1-inch cubes)

1 cups of frozen corn kernels

1 ½ cups of rice prepared according to directions on package (or better still 1 batch of my Cilantro Lime Rice)

1 tablespoon of olive oil

1 large bell pepper, diced (preferably green, red, yellow, or orange - whatever you like)

1 (about 15oz.) can black beans (rinsed and drained)

1 (about 20oz.) jar chunky salsa

¼ cup of water

Cilantro Lime Rice Ingredients

1 small lime

1-1/2 cup of white rice

¼ cup of chopped fresh cilantro

¼ teaspoon of salt (feel free to put additional salt to taste)

Optional accompaniments: avocado, fresh cilantro, sour cream, lime wedges, etc.

Directions

1. First, you heat oil over medium heat.
2. After which you add onions and bell peppers and cook for about 3-4 minutes until tender.
3. After that, you add chicken breast cubes and cook, stirring occasionally, until no visible pink remains on the outside (about 6-7 minutes).
4. Then you add in beans, corn, salsa, and water and bring to a simmer.
5. At this point, you reduce heat to medium-low and cover, stirring occasionally, for about 15 minutes until chicken is cooked through (NOTE: for a thicker sauce remove lid for the last 5 minutes of cooking.
6. Finally, you serve over rice and garnish with sour cream, fresh cilantro, avocado, etc.

Cilantro Lime Rice Directions

1. You are advice to prepare rice according to instructions on the package.
2. When the rice is finished, you add the juice from one salt, lime, and cilantro to the rice.
3. Then you stir and place back over low heat, uncovered for about 1 minute.

Tex Mex Turkey Loaf

Tips:

1. The spiciness of this recipe depends on the spiciness of the salsa you choose to use.
2. Feel free to add some shredded Cojack cheese to the mixture, but that would make it four ingredients!

Ingredients

2 eggs (beaten)

2 ½ lbs. of ground turkey

1 ¼ cups of salsa

½ teaspoon of pepper

½ teaspoon of salt

Preparation

1. First, you combine in a medium bowl, the salsa, pepper, and egg, salt and mix well.
2. After which you add ground turkey and combine.
3. After that, you form into a 12" round loaf.
4. Place loaf on a rack or balled up foil balls in a 3-quart crockpot.
5. Then you cover slow cooker and cook on low for about 4-5 hours, until turkey is thoroughly cooked and meat thermometer registers 160 degrees F.

Three Bean Cassoulet

TIP:
This recipe is a meatless low fat main dish, full of hearty beans and vegetables.

Ingredients

2 cups of dried great Northern beans

9 cups of water

2 onions (chopped)

2 tablespoons of dried parsley flakes

1 teaspoon of dried thyme leaves

¼ teaspoon of white pepper

4 tablespoons of tomato paste

2 cups of dried lima beans

2 cups of dried garbanzo beans

32 oz. bag baby carrots

6 garlic cloves (minced)

2 teaspoons of dried basil leaves

1 teaspoon of salt

2 bay leaves

28 oz. can diced tomatoes (undrained)

Preparation

1. First, you cover beans with cold water in large saucepan.
2. After which you bring to a boil for 1 minute.
3. After that, you remove from heat, cover, and let sit for 1 hour.
4. At this point, you drain beans and combine drained beans, 9 cups water, onion, carrots, garlic and seasonings except salt, tomatoes, and tomato paste in 5 quarts slow cooker.
5. This is when you mix well to combine.
6. Then you cover and cook on high heat for about 30 minutes.
7. Furthermore, you reduce heat to low and cook for about 8-9 hours or until beans and vegetables are tender.
8. After that, you stir in tomatoes, tomato paste, and salt, cover, and cook for 1 hour longer on low.
9. Finally, you remove bay leaf before serving.

Three Ingredient Crockpot Turkey

Note: remember there are different cooking times for this recipe, if you're using a bone-in or boneless breast.

Ingredients

One envelope dry onion soup mix

One frozen turkey breast, (not thawed) bone-in (5 pounds) or boneless (3 pounds)

1 lb. can cranberry sauce

Preparation

Directions for bone-in turkey

1. First, you put all ingredients into 5-6-quart crockpot.
2. After which you cover, and cook for 2 hours on high.
3. After that, you reduce heat to low and continue cooking for about 4-5 hours until turkey registers 170 degrees F on instant meat thermometer. (Note: Some sources now say that 165 degrees F is acceptable for a safe temperature).

Directions for boneless turkey breast

1. First, you follow instructions above.
2. After which you reduce the crockpot heat to low, start checking the turkey after 1-2 hours.
3. Remember, it may only need that much time to reach 170 degrees F.
4. Finally, you slice turkey breast and serve with sauce.

Turkey Breast Dijon

Ingredients

½ cup of Dijon mustard

¼ teaspoon of pepper

2 fresh bone-in turkey breast

1 ¼ cups of 100% fruit juice

2 teaspoons of salt

Preparation

1. First, you put turkey breast, skin side up, in 3-4 quart slow cooker.
2. After which you spread with Dijon mustard and season with salt and pepper to taste.
3. After that, you pour juice over the turkey and cover the crockpot.
4. Then you cook on low for about 8 to 9 hours, until turkey is tender and thoroughly cooked to 165 degrees F.

White Beans and Sun-Dried Tomatoes

Tip:
Remember, this delicious and creamy low fat crockpot recipe has flavors of the south of France.

Ingredients

6 cloves garlic (minced)

6 cups of vegetable broth

2 teaspoons of salt

1 teaspoon of Herbs de Provence

8 ounces can sliced black olives (drained)

1 cup of grated Parmesan cheese

4 cups of Great Northern beans (sorted)

2 onion (chopped)

6 cups of water

2 teaspoons of dried thyme leaves

1 ½ cups of chopped sun dried tomatoes in oil (drained)

2 cups of shredded Havarti cheese

Preparation

1. First, you mix all ingredients except tomatoes, olives, and cheeses in 3-4 quart slow cooker.

2. After which you cover slow cooker and cook on high for about 4-6 hours or until beans are tender.
3. After that, you mash some of the white beans while in the crockpot to thicken mixture.
4. Then you stir in tomatoes and olives and cook for 10 more minutes until thoroughly heated.
5. Finally, you stir in both types of cheese and serve.

Crockpot Greek Stew

Ingredients

2 cups of chopped carrots

1 cup of chopped zucchini

15 oz. of can garbanzo beans (rinsed and drained)

2 cloves garlic (minced)

½ teaspoon of salt

¼ teaspoon of pepper

½ cup of crumbled feta cheese

2 cups of cubed butternut squash

2 onions (chopped)

2 (about 14 oz.) cans diced tomatoes (undrained)

14 oz. of can vegetable broth

1 teaspoon of cumin

½ teaspoon of allspice

½ teaspoon of ground coriander

4 cups of hot cooked couscous

Preparation

1. First, you combine all ingredients except for couscous and cheese in a 3-4 quart slow cooker and mix well to combine.
2. After which you cover and cook on low for about 7 to 9 hours or until all vegetables are tender.
3. Then you serve with couscous and sprinkle with cheese.

Crockpot Sausage Stew

Ingredients

1 sweet potato (peeled and chopped)

2 onions (chopped)

1 lb. of smoked cooked sausage (sliced)

14 oz. of can diced tomatoes with seasonings (undrained)

½ teaspoon of salt

1 cup of water

½ cup of grated Parmesan cheese

1 russet potato (cut into 1/2" cubes)

16 oz. of bag baby carrots

2 cloves garlic (minced)

14 oz. of can ready to serve chicken broth

1 Tablespoon of sugar

1/8 teaspoon of pepper

½ teaspoon of dried thyme leaves

Preparation

1. First, you combine all ingredients except cheese in a 3-4-quart crockpot.

2. After which you cover slow cooker and cook on low for about 7-9 hours until vegetables are tender.
3. Then you serve with cheese.

BONUS RECIPES

Applesauce Kielbasa

Tips:

1. Remember to serve this super easy crockpot appetizer recipe at the start of a hearty fall meal.
2. You can use any fully-cooked sausage in place of the kielbasa if you'd like (NOTE: IF you'd like to make kielbasa at the last minute, I suggest you make Stove Apple Kielbasa)
3. You can also serve this as a main dish over some rice pilaf.

Ingredients

¾ cup of brown sugar

2 cloves garlic (minced)

2 lbs. of fully cooked kielbasa sausage

1 cup of chunky applesauce

2 Tablespoons of Dijon mustard

Preparation

1. First, you cut kielbasa into 1" pieces and combine with brown sugar, mustard, applesauce, and garlic in 3-quart crockpot.
2. After which you cover and cook on low for 6-8 hours until thoroughly heated.
3. Then if you have a new hot cooking crockpot, I suggest you cook on low for 4-6 hours until hot.

BBQ Beef Crockpot Sandwiches

Tips:

This recipe is a combination of 3 ingredients.

Ingredients

½ teaspoon of salt

¾ cup of barbecue sauce

2 lbs. of boneless beef round steak

¼ teaspoon of pepper

3 cups of purchased coleslaw mix (divided)

Preparation

1. First, you trim beef and cut into 1" pieces; sprinkle with salt and pepper.
2. After which you combine half of the coleslaw mix and barbecue sauce in medium bowl and mix to combine.
3. After that, you layer beef and coleslaw mixture in crockpot.
4. Then you cover crockpot and cook on low for about 7-9 hours until beef is tender.
5. At this point, you stir well with fork so beef falls apart.
6. Finally, you serve the cooked mixture in crusty sandwich buns, topped with the uncooked coleslaw mix.

BBQ Chicken Drummies

Tips:

1. Feel free to use your own barbecue sauce in this super easy five ingredient recipe.
2. Remember the spiciness of the finished dish will depend on the barbecue sauce hotness.

Ingredients

2 ½ cups of barbecue sauce

½ cup of honey

Dash pepper

6 lbs. chicken drummies (thawed if frozen)

4 tablespoons of chili sauce

6 cloves garlic (minced)

Preparation

1. First, you pat the chicken drummies dry with a paper towel and place on broiler pan.
2. After which you broil 5-6 inches from the heat for 8-10 minutes, turning often, until chicken is browned.
3. After that, you place in 6-quart crockpot.
4. At this point, you mix remaining ingredients in a small bowl and pour over drummies.
5. Finally, you cover and cook on low for about 4-5 hours until chicken is at 165 degrees F when measured with a meat thermometer.
6. However, these can be held for 1 hour after the cooking time on low.

Beach Boy's Pot Roast

Ingredients

Slivers of garlic

1 beef roast (chuck, top round, about $1.69/lb.)

Jar of pepperoncini peppers

Preparation

1. First, you cut some slits in roast and insert garlic slivers.
2. After which you place beef in crockpot.
3. After that, you dump peppers and all of the juice on top.
4. Then you crock all day on low....at least 12 hours.

Directions for serving:

1. First, you just slice and serve, or make BB's hoagies.
2. After which when it is cool, you fork-shred beef, spread on hoagie (sub) rolls, squirt on some Cheeze-Whiz and pig out!!!
3. Then you put some of those delicious (now meaty) pepperoncini peppers on the sub too!!

Cheesy Crockpot Chicken

Tips:

This recipe is delicious when served with hot cooked rice or couscous.

Ingredients

20 oz. of can condensed cream of chicken soup

4 teaspoons of chili powder

12 boneless, skinless chicken breasts

20 oz. of can condensed Fiesta cheese soup

¼ teaspoon of pepper

Preparation

1. First, you place chicken breasts in 7-quart crockpot.
2. After which you pour the undiluted soups over the chicken.
3. After that, you add the pepper and chili powder, and stir to combine.
4. Then you cover crockpot and cook on low for about 6 to 8 hours, until chicken is tender and thoroughly cooked.
5. Finally, you serve over rice or noodles.

Plant Paradox slow cooker cookbook

Crock Pot Cochinita Pibil

Ingredients
1 cup of orange juice
6 garlic cloves (diced)
2 tablespoons of coriander
2 teaspoons of dried oregano
1 cup of chicken broth
½ cup of cilantro for garnish

6 lbs. of pork shoulder (trimmed of fat)

4 habaneros (seeded and diced)

2 onions (chopped into quarters)
2 teaspoons of cumin

8 tablespoons of Achiote paste

Salt and pepper

1 cup of apple cider vinegar

Directions:

1. First, you season the pork shoulder with salt and pepper and rub with achiote paste.
2. After which you spread the bottom of the slow cooker with onions and garlic.
3. After that, you place the pork shoulder on top.
4. Then you combine the remaining ingredients in a bowl and pour over the pork shoulder.

5. At this point, you cook in your slow cooker for about 6-8 hours until the pork is fork tender.
6. This is when you pull the pork apart using a fork and mix together with the sauce.
7. Furthermore, you serve on its own, over rice, with a sandwich for a spicy pulled pork, or in tacos.
8. Finally, you garnish with freshly chopped cilantro.

NUTRITIONAL INFORMATION

Serving Size: about 6 ounce

Calories: 165

Fat: 7g

Carbs: 4.1g

Fiber: 1g

Creamy Crockpot Potatoes

Tips:

This simple Creamy Crockpot Potatoes makes for a wonderful rich and indulgent side dish; in your slow cooker!

Ingredients

About 8 oz. pkg. cream cheese (softened)

About 10 oz. can condensed cream of potato soup

About 2 lbs. of small red potatoes

1 envelope buttermilk ranch dry salad dressing mix

Preparation

1. First, you scrub potatoes and cut into quarters.
2. After which you place in a 3-4-quart crockpot.
3. After that, you combine cream cheese and salad dressing mix in small bowl and blend well.
4. Then you add condensed soup and mix well.
5. Furthermore, you pour over potatoes and cover crockpot.
6. Cook on low for about 7-9 hours until potatoes are tender.
7. Finally, you stir before serving.

Creamy Italian Chicken

Tips:

1. Remember that this simple and comforting recipe for Creamy Italian Chicken is not meant to be a gourmet treat.
2. This recipe is delicious and flavorful and perfect on a cold fall or winter night (note: I often add a package of baby carrots for more color and nutrition, also some chopped garlic is good too).

Ingredients

½ cup butter (melted)

2 teaspoons of dried chives

About 0.14-ounce package dry Italian Salad dressing mix

¼ teaspoon of pepper

4 pounds boneless, skinless chicken breasts

2 (8-ounce each) block cream cheese (softened, cut into cubes)

2 (10.75-ounce each) can condensed cream of onion soup

½ cup of water

2 teaspoons of dried Italian seasoning

Preparation

1. First, you cut chicken breasts into wide strips and place into a 3-4-quart crockpot.
2. After which you combine in a medium bowl melted butter, softened cream cheese, Italian dressing mix, soup, water, Italian seasoning, and pepper and stir until blended.
3. After that, you pour over chicken in crockpot.

4. At this point, you cover and cook on low for about 6-8 hours.
5. This is when you stir well, then serve over hot cooked pasta or rice.
6. If the sauce in this recipe isn't thick enough, I suggest you combine 4 tablespoons of cornstarch with 4 tablespoons of cold water and blend until smooth.
7. Furthermore, you stir into the crockpot and cook on high for about 10 minutes until the sauce thickens.
8. Feel free to add vegetables to this recipe to make it a one-dish meal and also a package of baby carrots, or a cup of chopped onion should be placed under the chicken and cooked for the full time.
9. In addition, you add sliced mushrooms to the crockpot in the last 2 hours.
10. Finally, you add sliced bell peppers or zucchini during the last hour of cooking.

Crockpot Pork with Cabbage

Tips:

The sweetness of the cabbage in this recipe really complements the juicy savory flavor of the pork roast.

Ingredients

2 onions (chopped)

1 1/3 cups of brown sugar

2 teaspoons of dried thyme leaves

7 pound of boneless pork shoulder roast

10 cups of shredded red cabbage

6 cloves garlic (minced)

1 1/3 cups of apple cider vinegar

1 teaspoon of salt

½ teaspoon of pepper

Preparation

1. First, you combine cabbage, brown sugar, onion, garlic, vinegar, and thyme in 4 to 5 quart slow cooker.
2. After which you sprinkle roast with salt and pepper and brown in heavy skillet, about 5-6 minutes total, turning until browned on all sides.

Plant Paradox slow cooker cookbook

(**NOTE:** you do not have to brown the pork if you don't want to; just sprinkle it with the salt and pepper and put it in the crockpot on top of the vegetables.)

3. Then you place pork in slow cooker; cover, and cook on Low for about 7-8 hours until pork registers 150 degrees F.
4. Finally, you remove pork from crockpot; cover and let stand for about 10 minutes before slicing to serve with the cabbage mixture.

Crockpot Chicken Supreme

Tips:

You are free to substitute different types of cheese and different flavors of condensed soup to change the flavor of this fabulous, easy slow cooker recipe for Crockpot Chicken Supreme.

Ingredients

12 boneless, skinless chicken breast halves

1 cup of diced Swiss (or preferably Havarti cheese)

10 slices bacon

20 oz. can condensed cream of chicken soup (OR better still 20 oz. jar four cheese Alfredo sauce)

8 oz. jar sliced mushrooms (drained OR better still 2 onions, chopped)

Preparation

1. First, you cook bacon in large skillet until crisp.
2. After which you remove bacon from skillet and drain on paper towels.
3. After that, you crumble bacon and set aside in refrigerator.
4. Furthermore, in bacon drippings in skillet, you cook chicken over medium heat for about 3-4 minutes or until light brown, turning once.
5. Then you place in a 4-6 quart slow cooker.
6. At this point, you top with mushrooms or onions (or both!).

7. This is when you heat in a skillet the soup, scraping up pan drippings, and pour over chicken in slow cooker.
8. In addition, you cover and cook on low setting for 4-5 hours, or until chicken registers 160°F on a meat thermometer.
9. After which you top chicken with diced cheese and sprinkle with bacon.
10. FINALLY, you cover and cook on high for about 10-15 minutes or until cheese is melted.

Note:

I recently started cooking this dish using frozen chicken breasts. I suggest you brown them, as directed, in the bacon drippings, then cook on low for 6-8 hours, until a food thermometer registers 160 degrees

Crockpot Sweet and Spicy Meatballs

Tips:

1. This recipe is so delicious and easier.
2. If you using your crockpot, all you have to do is stir occasionally (note: if you have any left to stir! Remember I myself think cocktail sauce is delicious with the jelly; it's basically just like chili sauce but a bit spicier).
3. Have in mind that any jelly or jam and any spicy tomato-based sauce works well for this recipe.

Ingredients

1 cups of grape (or preferably apple jelly)

2 cups of chili sauce (or preferably cocktail sauce)

2 pounds of precooked frozen meatballs (or better still your own homemade meatballs)

Preparation

1. First, you heat meatballs in oven as directed on package.
2. After which you place in 3-4-quart crockpot.
3. After that, you mix jelly and chili sauce or cocktail sauce thoroughly, pour over meatballs, stir well, cover crockpot, and heat on high 1-2 hours until sauce is hot.
4. Then you turn heat to low until ready to serve, stirring occasionally.

Crockpot Artichoke Spinach Dip

Ingredients

About 14 oz. of can marinated or preferably plain artichoke hearts, drained and chopped

½ cup of mayonnaise

1/8 teaspoon of pepper

1 (about 8-ounce) package cream cheese, cubed

1-1/2 cups of frozen cut leaf spinach

½ cup of purchased Alfredo sauce

¼ teaspoon of salt

1-1/2 cups of shredded Havarti cheese

Preparation

1. First, you thaw spinach and drain well, pressing to remove water.
2. After which you chop spinach and combine with rest of ingredients in a 2 quart slow cooker.
3. After that, you cover and cook on low setting for 2-3 hours.
4. Then you serve with crackers, toasted French bread, carrot sticks, and celery sticks.

Crockpot Beef and Black Eyed Pea Soup

Tips:

1. This recipe is a super hearty soup made with just four ingredients.
2. You could add a chopped onion or some minced garlic, if you wish.

Ingredients

12 carrots (peeled and chopped)

32 oz. pkg. dried black eyed peas

4 lb. beef chuck roast (cut into 2" cubes)

20 oz. can condensed bean and bacon soup

½ teaspoon of pepper

8 cups of water

Preparation

1. First, you sort through the black eyed peas to remove any stones or shriveled peas, then rinse and drain.
2. After which you combine all ingredients in 4-5-quart crockpot.
3. Then you cover and cook on low for about 9-10 hours or until peas are tender and beef is done.

Crockpot Chili Beef Sandwiches

Tip:

Make sure you sprinkle some grated cheese on these delicious Crockpot Chili Beef Sandwiches.

Ingredients

8 Kaiser Rolls (split and toasted)

3 lb. of boneless beef chuck roast

1 pkg. of taco seasoning mix (or 2 Tablespoons of Homemade Taco Seasoning Mix)

2 cups of barbecue sauce

Preparation

1. First, you trim excess fat from beef and brown beef on all sides in heavy skillet over medium high heat.
2. After which you transfer to 4-5 quart slow cooker.
3. After that, you sprinkle with seasoning mix and pour sauce over.
4. Then you cover and cook on low for about 8-10 hours.
5. Furthermore, you remove beef from crockpot and shred; return to crockpot.
6. Finally, you make sandwiches with Kaiser Rolls.

Crockpot Chili con Queso

Tip:

Feel free to use spicy or mild products for this easy Crockpot Chili con Queso appetizer recipe

Ingredients

1-1/2 cups of chunky salsa

1/8 teaspoon of cayenne pepper

1 lb. pkg. Mexican or plain pasteurized process cheese spread

4 oz. can chopped green chilies (or better still minced jalapenos, drained)

¼ teaspoon of pepper

Preparation

1. First, you combine all ingredients in 3-4-quart crockpot.
2. After which you cover and cook on low for 2 to 2-1/2 hours or until cheese is melted, stirring twice during cooking.
3. Then you remove the lid from the crockpot and cook on high for 1 hour longer, until mixture is hot.

Crockpot Chutney Ham

Tips:

1. Remember that this super easy dinner recipe for ham cooked in the crockpot has the most wonderful flavor.
2. Make sure you serve it for your next dinner party, or for the perfect Easter or Christmas dinner.

Ingredients

¼ teaspoon of pepper

1 Tablespoon of balsamic vinegar

3 lb. of fully cooked boneless ham

2 (about 6 oz.) jars mango chutney

1 onion (chopped)

Preparation

1. First, you place ham in crockpot.
2. After which you mix remaining ingredients in a medium bowl and pour over the ham.
3. Then you cover crockpot and cook on low for 6-8 hours until thoroughly heated.

NUTRITIONAL INFORMATION

Serving Size: per serving

Calories: 370
Fat: 16 grams
Sodium: 2000 mg

Crockpot Crab Spread

Ingredients

8 oz. pkg. cream cheese (softened)

1 lb. lump crabmeat (picked over to remove cartilage and shell bits)

¾ cup of mayonnaise

2 Tablespoons of apple juice

1 onion (minced)

Preparation

1. First, you mix mayonnaise, cream cheese, and apple juice in medium bowl until blended.
2. After that, you place in 1 - 3-quart crockpot.
3. Then you stir in onions and blend well.
4. At this point, you gently stir in crabmeat.
5. Furthermore, you cover crockpot and cook on LOW for 4 hours.
6. At this point the dip will hold for up to 2 hours, stirring occasionally.

Crockpot Easiest Pork Chops

Ingredients

20 oz. can ready to serve chicken broth

8 pork chops (well-trimmed)

2 envelope onion soup mix

Preparation

1. Brown the pork chops if you wish in a nonstick skillet, 3-4 minutes on each side.
2. After that, you place pork chops in 3-1/2-4-quart crockpot.
3. Then you combine soup mix and chicken broth in medium bowl and stir until blended.
4. After which, you pour this mixture over the pork chops.
5. Finally, you cover crockpot and cook on low heat for 6 to 8 hours.

Crockpot Fish Chowder

Tips:
1. This hearty recipe is full of rich flavors.
2. Feel free to use any firm fleshed fish you'd like.

Ingredients

1 green bell pepper (chopped)

3 cloves garlic (minced)

2 cups eight vegetable juice (V8)

1 Tablespoon of Worcestershire sauce

¼ teaspoon of crushed red pepper flakes

½ cup of uncooked instant rice

2 Tablespoons of grated Parmesan cheese

2 celery stalks (chopped)

1 onion (chopped)

2 (about 14 oz.) cans diced tomatoes (undrained)

1 cup of vegetable broth (or better still fish stock)

½ teaspoon of salt

1 lb. of firm fish steaks (such as haddock, swordfish, halibut, salmon), cut into 1" pieces

¼ cup of chopped fresh parsley

1 teaspoon of grated lemon peel

Preparation

1. First, you mix all ingredients except rice, fish, parsley, lemon peel and Parmesan cheese in a 3-5 quart slow cooker.
2. After which you cover crockpot and cook on low for about 6-7 hours (high setting 3-4 hours) until vegetables are tender.
3. After that, you stir in fish and rice.
4. Then you cover crockpot and cook on high setting for about 30-45 minutes until fish flakes easily when tested with a fork.
5. In the meantime, you combine in small bowl parsley, lemon peel, and cheese and mix to blend.
6. Finally, you serve this topping with stew.

Crockpot Fruited Pork

Tips:
This is the most wonderful rich and hearty pork dinner recipe.

Ingredients

1-1/2 cups of mixed dried fruit including apricots

2 Tablespoons of apple cider vinegar

¼ teaspoon of pepper

2-3 lb. of pork boneless loin roast

1 cup of apricot nectar

2 teaspoons of curry powder

½ teaspoon of salt

Preparation

1. First, you place pork in 3-4 quart slow cooker and top with fruit.
2. After which you pour apple juice and vinegar over pork and sprinkle with curry powder, salt, and pepper.
3. After that, you cover crockpot and cook on low for about 7-9 hours until pork is tender.
4. Finally, if you have a new, hotter cooking crockpot, I suggest you check the pork after 6 hours on low.

Crockpot Gingered Carrots

Tips:

This super simple recipe is packed full of flavor and is perfect for holiday menus.

Ingredients

1/3 cup of Dijon mustard

1 tablespoon of minced ginger root

½ teaspoon of salt

12 carrots (peeled and sliced)

½ cup of brown sugar

1/8 teaspoon of pepper

Preparation

1. First, you combine all ingredients in 3-4-quart crockpot.
2. After which you cover and cook on high for about 2-3 hours or until carrots are tender, stirring twice during cooking.

NUTRITIONAL INFORMATION

Serving Size: per serving

Calories: 70
Fat: 0 grams
Sodium: 174 mg

Crockpot Ham Lentil Stew

Tip:

This simple stew recipe cooks all day in your crockpot.

Ingredients

3 cups of carrots (chopped)

2 onions (chopped)

4 cups of water

3 cups of cooked ham (chopped)

2 cups of dried lentils (sorted and rinsed)

2 (about 10 oz.) cans condensed chicken broth

Preparation

1. First, you combine all ingredients in 3-4 quart slow cooker and mix to combine.
2. Then you cover crockpot and cook on low for about 7-9 hours.

Crockpot Honey BBQ Pork and Carrots

Tips:

1. However, if you'd like you could add a chopped onion or two and some minced garlic.
2. Make sure you serve this meal with some hot cooked brown rice mixed with some chopped parsley or cilantro.
3. Furthermore, this simple green salad with a blue cheese dressing would be a fabulous side dish.

Ingredients

32 oz. bag baby carrots

½ cup of honey

½ teaspoon of pepper

6 lb. of boneless pork roast

1 cup of purchased barbecue sauce

1 teaspoon of salt

Preparation

1. First, you place pork and carrots in a 3-4-quart crockpot.
2. After which you combine barbecue sauce, honey, salt and pepper in a small bowl and pour over ingredients in crockpot.
3. Then you cover and cook on low for about 8-10 hours or pork is thoroughly cooked.

NUTRITIONAL INFORMATION

Serving Size: per serving

Plant Paradox slow cooker cookbook

Calories: 550
Fat: 23 grams
Sodium: 800 mg
Vitamin A: 100% DV

Crockpot Honey Chicken and Dried Fruit

Tips:

1. I cherish this combination of chicken with dried fruit.
2. Remember, that this dried fruit combines with the honey, broth, and vinegar to make a delicious chutney that pairs perfectly with the tender chicken.

Ingredients

½ teaspoon of ground ginger

¼ teaspoon of pepper

½ cup of honey

1 onion (chopped)

8 boneless, skinless chicken thighs

½ teaspoon of salt

1 cup of mixed dried fruit pieces

1/3 cup of chicken broth

2 tablespoons of apple cider vinegar

Preparation

1. First, you place all ingredients in 4-5 quart slow cooker.
2. After which you cover and cook on low for about 8-9 hours until chicken is tender and thoroughly cooked.
3. Then you serve over hot cooked rice or egg noodles.

NOTE:

Plant Paradox slow cooker cookbook

1. Make sure you do not use bone-in pieces of chicken because the recipe may not work. Remember, bone-in dark meat chicken, cooks very differently from boneless in the crockpot.

Crockpot Hungarian Goulash

Tips:

1. Remember, this isn't a 100% traditional goulash, but the basic flavors are here.
2. I prefer to serve it on a bed of sautéed cabbage strips, Cauliflower "rice" works well, too.
3. To turn it from a goulash to a paprikash, I suggest you serve with a glob of sour cream on the top, and each person can stir their own in.
4. Make sure you have the butcher cut up the meat and take off excess fat.

Ingredients

It is Optional: up to ¼ of the meat can be ham, for a smokier taste

2 medium red Bell peppers (chopped)

4 cloves garlic

1 teaspoon of hot Hungarian Paprika (or better still ½ teaspoon hot red pepper)

1 teaspoon of caraway seed

Salt and pepper

3 lbs. of pork shoulder, trimmed of fat and cut into ~1½-inch cubes (make sure you have the butcher do this)

2 cups of onions (thinly sliced)

6 medium stalks celery (chopped)

6 Tablespoons of sweet Hungarian paprika

1 teaspoon of marjoram

2 bay leaves

¼ cup of tomato paste

Preparation

1. First, you season the pork with salt and pepper, and brown in a skillet over medium-high heat.

NOTE: Browning is not essential, but takes out more excess fat and some of the moisture, as well as adding flavor. (But if you're using ham, do not cook it on the stove.)

2. After that, you put in the bottom of the crockpot.
3. Then you sauté the vegetables in a skillet over high heat for about 3 to 5 minutes to remove some moisture.
4. Furthermore, you remove from heat, and add the rest of the ingredients and combine well.
5. After which you spoon into crockpot over the meat.
6. At this point, you cook for about 3 hours on high, or 6 to 8 hours on low.
7. Then about half an hour before serving, taste and adjust seasonings.

NUTRITIONAL INFORMATION

Serving Size:

Calories: 241

Fat: 3g

Carbs: 5g

Plant Paradox slow cooker cookbook

Fiber: 3g

Protein: 28g

Italian Chicken and Potatoes

Tips:

1. Feel free to add other ingredients to this super easy recipe (For me I did add a chopped onion and some baby carrots.)

Ingredients

1 cup of zesty Italian salad dressing

1 teaspoon of dried Italian seasoning

8 potatoes (cubed)

3 lbs. of boneless, skinless chicken breasts, sliced

¼ teaspoon of pepper

8 cloves garlic (minced)

Preparation

1. First, you combine all ingredients in a 3-4-quart crockpot.
2. Then you cover and cook on low for about 6-8 hours until chicken is thoroughly cooked and potatoes are tender.

Crockpot Italian Pork Chops

Ingredients

Salt and pepper to taste

2 onion (chopped)

2 cups of shredded mozzarella cheese

12 (1" thick) boneless pork loin chops

2 tablespoons of olive oil

6 cloves garlic (minced)

6 cups of chunky pasta sauce

Preparation

1. First, you trim any excess fat from pork chops and sprinkle with salt and pepper.
2. After which you cook chops in olive oil in a heavy skillet over medium heat for about 3-4 minutes until browned, turning once during cooking.
3. After that, you place in 3-4 quart slow cooker.
4. Then you add onions and garlic to drippings; cook for 5 minutes, then add to slow cooker.
5. At this point, you top with pasta sauce.
6. This is when you cover with crockpot and cook on low for about 7-9 hours until pork is tender and thoroughly cooked.
7. Furthermore, you remove pork from slow cooker and stir in 24 ounces cooked and drained fettuccine.
8. Finally, you place fettuccine on serving platter; top with chops, then with cheese just before serving.

NUTRITIONAL INFORMATION

Serving Size: per serving

Calories: 420
Fat: 16 grams
Sodium: 700 mg

Chicken Tikka Masala Pizza

SERVES: 2 9in pizzas

Ingredients:

Ingredients for Pizza Topping:

2 cup of strained tomatoes (or tomato sauce)

2 garlic cloves (minced)

1 teaspoon of dried ginger

1 teaspoon of salt

½ cup of cashew cream

½ cup of fresh cilantro (chopped)

1 lb. of chicken thighs (skinless and boneless)

½ yellow onion (chopped)

2½ tablespoons of garam masala powder

½ teaspoon of paprika

Pinch of cayenne pepper

1 cup of smoked gouda cheese, shredded (it is optional)

Crust

½ cup of coconut flour

- 2 teaspoons of curry powder
- ¾ teaspoon of salt
- ⅓ cup of extra-virgin olive oil
- 1 teaspoon of apple cider vinegar
- 1½ cups of whole raw cashews
- ¼ cup plus 2 tablespoons of almond flour
- 1 teaspoon of baking soda
- 4 eggs
- ½ cup of almond milk
- 2 tablespoons of cold water

Cashew Cream:

- 1 cup of raw cashews

Directions:

1. First, you mix the tomato sauce, garam masala, onions, garlic, ginger, paprika, salt, and cayenne pepper.
2. After which you pour it into the insert of a slow cooker.
3. After that, you place the chicken on top of the sauce and cook on low for 6 hours.
4. When the sauce has 30 minutes left to cook, you now preheat your oven to about 350 degrees.

5. Furthermore, in a food processor, you grind the cashews until a fine flour has formed.
6. After that, you add the almond flour, coconut flour, baking soda, salt, and curry powder, then process the mixture for 1 minute.
7. At this point, you add the eggs, almond milk, apple cider vinegar, olive oil, and water and process for another minute.
8. This is when you scrape down the sides of the bowl and pulse a few more times until you have a very smooth dough.
9. After which you let the dough rest for 2 minutes to let the coconut flour absorb some of the liquid.
10. Then you sprinkle a piece of parchment paper with a little almond flour, then turn the dough out onto the counter.
11. In addition, you sprinkle a little more flour on the top of the ball of dough, then place another piece of parchment on top.
12. Make use of your hands to flatten the ball into a disc, then lightly roll out the dough into a circle that is ¼ inch thick.
13. After that, you carefully remove the top piece of parchment (You may have to gently tug from the corner to get the parchment to release as it is a sticky dough).
14. This is the point; you slide the other piece with the crust onto a pizza pan.
15. Bake the crust for about 12 minutes, or until it has puffed up slightly and is golden brown around the edges.
16. While the crust is baking, I suggest you remove the chicken from the sauce and give it a rough chop.
17. At this point, you remove the sauce from the heat and stir in the cashew cream.
18. Return the chicken back to the sauce and brush the crust with a little olive oil, then spoon the chicken and sauce onto the pre-baked pizza crusts, leaving a ½ border of crust.
19. Finally, you sprinkle with cheese, then return to the oven and bake for another 15 minutes until the cheese has melted.

20. Make sure you sprinkle with fresh cilantro and serve hot.

Directions to Make the Cashew Cream

1. First, you soak 1 cup of raw cashews in 3 cups hot water for about 30 minutes.
2. After which you drain the cashews, but reserve the soaking water.
3. Then you place the cashews in a blender with ¾ cup of the soaking water and blend until smooth (NOTE: It should be a similar thickness of a Greek yogurt. If it's too thick, I suggest you add a little water at a time to get your desired consistency.)

Crockpot Italian Sausage and Peppers Recipes

Tip: this recipe is a super easy and flavorful and you can cook it all day while you're busy doing other things.

Ingredients

2 yellow onions (chopped)

1 red bell pepper (cut into 2" pieces)

2 bay leaves

14 oz. of can diced tomatoes (undrained)

½ cup of dry red wine or better still water

½ teaspoon of dried oregano leaves

1/8 teaspoon of white pepper

2 lbs. of sweet or better still hot Italian turkey sausage

1 orange bell pepper (cut into 2" pieces)

1 yellow bell pepper (cut into 2" pieces)

4 cloves garlic (minced)

6 oz. of can tomato paste

1 Tablespoon of dried parsley leaves

½ teaspoon of dried basil leaves

½ teaspoon of salt

Preparation

1. First, you cook turkey sausage in heavy skillet over medium heat until browned, turning occasionally.
2. After which you layer half of the onions on bottom of 3-4-quart crockpot, then add half of the peppers.
3. After that, you add all of the browned turkey sausage, then the rest of the onions and peppers.
4. Then you add bay leaves and garlic.
5. At this point, you combine diced undrained tomatoes, tomato paste, and red wine in small bowl and mix well to blend.
6. Furthermore, you pour over mixture in crockpot.
7. After which you cover slow cooker and cook on low for about 6 hours.
8. Remember, one hour before mixture is done, I suggest you mix together parsley, basil, oregano, and salt and pepper.
9. After that, you add to crockpot and stir well.
10. Finally, you cover and cook one more hour until sausage is thoroughly cooked and vegetables are tender.

Crockpot Maple Glazed Turkey Breast

Tip:

This recipe is delicious with a cornbread stuffing that cooks right along with the turkey.

Ingredients

2 onions (chopped)

1 teaspoon of salt

6-8 pound of boneless turkey breast (thawed if frozen)

1 cup of apricot preserves

Salt and pepper to taste

4 tablespoons of butter

2 (8" x 8") pan cornbread, crumbled

¼ teaspoon of pepper

2/3 cup of maple syrup

6 tablespoons of butter (melted)

1 teaspoon of dried thyme leaves

Preparation

1. First, you melt butter in small saucepan.
2. After which you cook onion until very tender.
3. After that, you remove to large bowl and crumble in cornbread.
4. Then you season with 1 teaspoon salt and ¼ teaspoon pepper.

5. At this point, you sprinkle turkey breast with more salt and pepper.
6. Furthermore, you combine in a small bowl the maple syrup, apricot preserves, butter, thyme leaves, and salt and pepper to taste; mix well.
7. After that, you add half this mixture to the cornbread mixture; place in 4-5 quart slow cooker.
8. This is when you place turkey on top and pour remaining maple syrup mixture over.
9. Finally, you cover and cook on low for about 6-7 hours until the turkey registers a temperature 165 degrees on a meat thermometer, basting twice with the juices in the crockpot.
10. Make sure you serve immediately.

Crockpot Mexican Flank Steak

Tips:

1. Remember that this savory, low fat crockpot entree combines flank steak with Mexican flavors (NOTE: not all Mexican food is super-spicy, but this one is).
2. If you like hot food, I suggest you add a habanero pepper or cayenne pepper to the recipe.
3. Have it at the back of your mind that the crockpot tends to mute flavors, so I suggest you add more oregano or other ingredients to the recipe at the very end if you'd like.

Ingredients

12 canned or better still fresh tomatillos

2 red onion (chopped)

2 teaspoons of salt

2 teaspoons of dried oregano

5 lb. of beef flank steak

28 oz. can whole baby corn on the cob (drained)

6 cloves garlic (minced)

¼ teaspoon of pepper

28 oz. can diced tomatoes (undrained)

½ cup of chopped fresh cilantro

Preparation

1. First, you trim flank steak to remove any visible fat.
2. After which you remove husk and stem from tomatillos, if necessary, and chop.
3. After that, you place drained corn on the cob, onion, and garlic in the bottom of 3 quarts slow cooker.
4. Then you top with steak and tomatillos.
5. At this point, you sprinkle all with salt, oregano, pepper, and cilantro.
6. Furthermore, you pour diced tomatoes over.
7. After that, you cover crockpot and cook on low for about 6-7 hours or until steak is tender.
8. Then you remove steak and slice crosswise across grain into strips.
9. Finally, you season the sauce to taste and serve vegetables and sauce with steak.

Crockpot Mexican Round Steak

Ingredients

4 cups of frozen corn (thawed and drained)

24 oz. can black beans (rinsed and drained)

1 cup of water

¼ teaspoon of crushed red pepper flakes

3 lbs. boneless beef round steak

36 oz. jar chunky garden salsa

2 onion (chopped)

1 teaspoon of salt

Preparation

1. First, you cut beef into 12 serving-size pieces and trim excess fat.
2. After which you place in a 3-4 quart slow cooker.
3. After that, you mix remaining ingredients in a medium bowl and pour over beef.
4. Then you cover crockpot and cook on low for about 8-9 hours until beef is tender.
5. Finally, if you have a new hotter cooking crockpot, I suggest you check the beef after 5-1/2 hours on low.

Crockpot Moroccan Lentil Stew

Tip:

However, with the combination of lentils, potatoes, and squash simmer in your slow cooker, it will result in a delicious meatless Crockpot Moroccan Lentil Stew.

Ingredients

2 lb. of butternut squash (peeled and cubed)

2 onion (chopped)

4 (about 28 oz.) cans diced tomatoes, undrained

2 teaspoons of cumin

¼ teaspoon of white pepper

4 cups of water

16 oz. pkg. frozen cut green beans (thawed)

2 cups of dried lentils (sorted and rinsed)

20 small new red potatoes (cubed)

8 cloves garlic (minced)

2 tablespoons of curry powder

1 teaspoon of salt

¼ teaspoon of crushed red pepper

4 tablespoons of lemon juice

2-4 teaspoons of curry powder

Preparation

1. First, you combine all ingredients except lemon juice, curry powder, and green beans in a 4-5 quart slow cooker.
2. After which you cover and cook on low for about 7-8 hours until lentils, squash, and potatoes are tender when tested with knife.
3. After that, you increase heat to high setting.
4. Then you stir in lemon juice mixed with the second amount of curry powder, and thawed green beans.
5. At this point, you cover and cook for about 10-15 minutes until mixture is thoroughly heated and beans are tender.
6. Furthermore, if you have a new hotter cooking crockpot cook on low for about 6-8 hours until lentils and potatoes are tender.
7. In the other hand, if the recipe is 'mush' you cooked it too long and always season food to taste.
8. Finally, as I have explained before, the crockpot mute's spices, so you may need to add more curry powder and cumin before serving.

Crockpot Onion Meatballs

Tip:

This delicious and super easy appetizer recipe uses just four ingredients.

Ingredients

1 envelope dry onion soup mix

About 10 oz. jar beef gravy

1/8 teaspoon of pepper

3 lbs. of frozen cooked meatballs

3 cloves garlic (minced)

3 Tablespoons of water

Preparation

1. First, you combine all ingredients in 4 - 6-quart crockpot.
2. After which you stir to combine.
3. Then you cover crockpot and cook on LOW for about 4-5 hours until thoroughly heated.

Crockpot Onion Turkey with Stuffing

Tip:
This simple crockpot recipe is a good Thanksgiving dinner for a small gathering.

Ingredients

2 onion (chopped)

12 oz. pkg. of turkey flavor stuffing mix (one step brand)

Salt and pepper to taste

2 tablespoons of olive oil

4 tablespoons of apple jelly

1 ½ cups of water

4 lb. of boneless, skinless turkey breast half

Preparation

1. First, you heat oil in a large skillet.
2. After which you add onion and cook for about 5 minutes until light brown, stirring frequently.
3. After that, you add jelly and heat for 1 minute longer or until golden brown.
4. Then you spray a 4-6 quart slow cooker with nonstick cooking spray.
5. At this point, you place stuffing mix in prepared cooker.
6. Furthermore, you drizzle with water and mix gently.
7. After that, you sprinkle turkey with salt and pepper and place on stuffing mix.

8. This is when you spoon onion mixture over turkey and spread evenly.
9. Finally, you cover and cook on low for about 5-6 hours.

Crockpot Peanut Chicken

Tip:

This super simple recipe is packed full of flavor.

Ingredients

1 cup of peanut butter

2 cups of chicken broth

4 tablespoons of brown sugar

½ teaspoon of garlic powder

6 pounds boneless, skinless chicken breasts

1 cup of orange juice

½ cup of low sodium soy sauce

2 teaspoon of ground ginger

¼ teaspoon of pepper

Preparation

1. First, you combine all ingredients in 4-quart crockpot; mix well.
2. After which you cover and cook on low for about 5-8 hours or until chicken is tender and thoroughly cooked.
3. After that, you serve with hot cooked rice or noodles.
4. Then if you have a newer hotter cooking crockpot, I suggest you check the chicken after 4-1/2 hours.
5. Remember the peanut butter can burn easily, so keep an eye on it.

Crockpot Pork Chili

Tips:

Make sure you use your favorite salsa in this super easy recipe (NOTE: a hot salsa will make the chili spicier).

If you like really hot food, I suggest you add a chopped jalapeno pepper.

Ingredients

2 onion (chopped)

24-oz. jar thick and chunky salsa

¼ teaspoon of cayenne pepper

2 green bell pepper (chopped)

4 pounds' boneless pork shoulder (cut into 1" pieces)

30-oz. can chunky tomato sauce

2 tablespoons of chili powder

1 teaspoon of oregano

½ teaspoon of salt

Preparation

1. First, you combine all ingredients except green pepper in 3-5 quart slow cooker.
2. After which you cover and cook on low for about 8-10 hours until pork is tender.
3. After that, you add bell pepper, increase heat to high, and cook for about 15-20 minutes longer.

4. Then if you have a newer, hotter cooking crockpot, I suggest you check the pork for doneness after 6-7 hours.

CONCLUSION

Thanks for reading through this book; if you follow judiciously the recipes outlined above, you will sleep better, feel better, think better, have more energy and loss weight without effort.

Remember, the only bad action you can take is no action at all.

www.ingramcontent.com/pod-product-compliance
Lightning Source LLC
Chambersburg PA
CBHW081721100526
44591CB00016B/2449